THE THIRD JIHAD

THE

THIRD

JIHAD

Overcoming Radical Islam's Plan for the West

MICHAEL YOUSSEF

TYNDALE
MOMENTUM®

The nonfiction imprint of
Tyndale House Publishers, Inc.

Visit Tyndale online at www.tyndale.com.

Visit Tyndale Momentum online at www.tyndalemomentum.com.

TYNDALE, Tyndale Momentum, and Tyndale's quill logo are registered trademarks of Tyndale House Publishers, Inc. The Tyndale Momentum logo is a trademark of Tyndale House Publishers, Inc. Tyndale Momentum is the nonfiction imprint of Tyndale House Publishers, Inc., Carol Stream, Illinois.

The Third Jihad: Overcoming Radical Islam's Plan for the West

Published in association with Don Gates of the literary agency The Gates Group; www.gatesliterary.com.

For information about special discounts for bulk purchases, please contact Tyndale House Publishers at csresponse@tyndale.com, or call 1-800-323-9400.

ISBN 978-1-4964-3150-9

Printed in the United States of America

25	24	23	22	21	20	19
7	6	5	4	3	2	1

CONTENTS

1

THE ISLAMIC STATES OF AMERICA

AN AMERICAN ISLAMIST IMAM in Washington, DC, has called for the creation of an Islamic State of North America by 2050—that is, imposing a theocratic totalitarian government across the United States, Mexico, and Canada. No one takes his prediction seriously. No one thinks it could ever happen here.

But instead of shaking our heads and laughing off such an "unthinkable" notion, perhaps we should pause and prayerfully ask, "*Could* it happen here?"

Many big moments in history were unthinkable—until they happened.

Could fifty-two American embassy employees be held hostage for more than fourteen months by a group of college students?

Unthinkable.

But it happened in Iran in 1979.

Could eight hundred thousand people be slaughtered in the span of one hundred days by soldiers, former friends, and neighbors?

Unthinkable.

But it happened in Rwanda in 1994.

Could nineteen men hijack four commercial airliners and fly them into three buildings and an open field, killing nearly three thousand people and injuring six thousand more?

Unthinkable.

But it happened in America in 2001.

Perhaps more to the point, could a Western democracy fall into the hands of a ruthless dictator "in part by using democratic freedoms to undermine and then destroy democracy itself"?[1]

Unthinkable.

No one likes comparisons to Nazi Germany, but it happened there in 1933, and the seeds are being sown for it to happen again—only this time with an Islamist government—across Europe, Great Britain, and even North America.

As we'll see, an Islamic State of North America is not unthinkable to the Islamists. They are planning for it and patiently working toward it, day by day. The choices we make now, and in the years to come, in America and across Western civilization, will either pave the way for the unthinkable or stop the Islamists in their tracks.

It's time we pause and think about the unthinkable. The Third Jihad has already begun—a holy war conducted not only with terror and violence, but also by stealth and intimidation. Like the two jihads that came before it—the wars of Islamic conquest (622–751) and the wars of Islamic expansion (1302–1922)—the Third Jihad demands a strong response.

What if the imam is right?

Because I was born in 1948, it is statistically unlikely that I will live to see the year 2050. But my children, grandchildren, and great-grandchildren can reasonably expect to be alive in that year—and the same can probably be said of yours.

But what will America look like in 2050?

If the imam in Washington has his way, every man, woman, and child within the present-day borders of Canada, the United States, and Mexico will live under the authority of the Islamic State of North America. As the founder of an Islamist organization with branches in Washington, Philadelphia, and four California cities, he is actively working toward this goal.[2]

His role model is the late Ayatollah Khomeini, the Shia Muslim cleric who led the 1979 Iranian Revolution that overthrew the 2,500-year-old Persian monarchy and established the Islamic Republic of Iran. Why does this American imam revere the Ayatollah Khomeini? I believe it's because Khomeini achieved in Iran the same goal the imam is pursuing in America: a cultural revolution and the establishment of a theocratic Islamic state.

As the imam told his followers in 2008, "Our quest is to emulate the life of our hero in contemporary times, Imam Khomeini, as we strive to establish the Islamic State of North America. His story is a story of ultimate success against unbelievable odds."[3]

You might think that what this Muslim leader envisions—an

Islamic-ruled America—is simply impossible. It could never happen. But just suppose for a moment that the Islamists managed to achieve their goals. Imagine what life in America would be like under Islamic rule.

A preventable future

A famous science-fiction writer once said that he wrote futuristic stories not to *predict* the future, but to *prevent* it.[4] The scenario you are about to read is not a prediction—at least I hope not. But it *is* a wake-up call. I hope what you're about to read will inspire you to help prevent this future from ever coming to pass.

Let's jump forward to the year 2050. The Islamic State of North America (ISNA) is now firmly in control of the US government and all the institutions of American society.

At first glance, the September 11 memorial in lower Manhattan looks much as it has since it was dedicated in 2011. Two square pools of water still mark the footprint of the World Trade Center towers that collapsed during the 2001 terror attacks.

But a closer look reveals big changes. The Cross at Ground Zero, a formation of steel beams resembling the Christian cross that was found in the World Trade Center debris, has been removed from the memorial museum. The names of those who died in the attacks have also been removed, replaced by a marble tablet inscribed with just nineteen names—the nineteen al-Qaeda "martyrs" who hijacked the planes and flew them into the towers, the Pentagon, and the grassy field in Pennsylvania.

The Islamist regime has altered some American monuments and destroyed others. Just as the Taliban dynamited the centuries-old Bamiyan Buddhas in Afghanistan in March 2001, the rulers of the American caliphate have dynamited great symbols of American freedom—the Statue of Liberty, Mount Rushmore, and the Lincoln Memorial. The Supreme Islamic Council of America, in a televised ceremony, brought out the original parchments of the Declaration of Independence, the Constitution, and the Bill of Rights, and fed them to a bonfire in front of the National Archives.

As an Islamist imam in Denmark once declared, "No Muslim can accept secularism, freedom, and democracy. It is for Allah alone to legislate how society shall be regulated! Muslims wish and long for Allah's law to replace the law of man."[5] In 2050, the Islamists' dream has come true in America, as Sharia law replaces the Constitution and other founding documents of the United States.

Just as in the days when ISIS controlled much of Iraq and Syria, ISNA has decreed that all property belonging to heretical religious groups—Christian churches, Jewish synagogues, and even "apostate" Islamic sects—shall be subject to confiscation. Cathedrals, churches, and synagogues are being shuttered or converted to mosques.

Your adult children have been ordered to renounce Jesus and convert to Islam or pay the *jizya*, the tax of submission to Islam. Your granddaughters have been taken out of school and sent home because girls need to learn only one thing: obedient submission. Any female found outside the home unaccompanied by a male relative, and without being covered from head to toe, risks brutal punishment.

Department stores and dress shops that once offered the

latest colorful fashions for women now offer only shades of black, brown, and white. Stores sell only niqabs (cloth coverings for a woman's face and hair) and robe-like chadors. ISNA billboards around the city depict fully veiled, robed women, and warn that women who do not properly cover themselves face fines and imprisonment.

Your grandsons, as young as fourteen years old, have been conscripted as fighters in the Muslim army, just as the Islamic State in Iraq and Syria once conscripted young boys into its army. Your grandsons must swear allegiance to the Islamic State, and they will be taught to root out secret enclaves of Christians, Jews, and other "infidels" and "idolaters," and to wage jihad against apostates and heretics of rival Muslim sects.

Not that life under the Islamic State is all bad. There are some good things to be said for a theocratic dictatorship. Just as ISIS was once a model of bureaucratic efficiency during its occupation of Iraq and Syria, ISNA has vastly improved government efficiency in 2050. Under the old American government, strong unions and federal regulations made it almost impossible to fire or discipline government workers who didn't do their jobs. In ISNA, government workers no longer slack off or go on strike because the regime will imprison them (or worse) if they fail to achieve their quotas.

The brutally efficient ISNA bureaucracy collects the garbage, sweeps the streets, fixes the potholes, maintains power lines and cell phone towers, keeps the tap water flowing, prevents the sewers from backing up, and collects the taxes. ISNA levies taxes on every conceivable transaction, and their collectors extract payment from the citizenry with a ruthlessness that makes Americans nostalgic for the kindly benevolence of the Internal Revenue Service.

In 2050, your children and grandchildren will need a strong stomach to handle the daily roadside death scenes staged by the ISNA's Diwan Al-Hisbah—the Ministry of Moral Code Enforcement. Most Islamic-ruled nations maintain a paid or volunteer force to enforce Sharia law. Islamist America will be no different. In Saudi Arabia, this force is called the Mutaween. In Iran, it is called the Guidance Patrol (Gasht-e Ershad). In the English-speaking ISNA, this force is known simply as the Morality Police.

Often working undercover, the Morality Police patrol the streets, parks, shopping malls, grocery stores, and schools, making sure that women obey the dress codes, men obey the haircut and beard regulations, children are quiet and reverent during the call to prayer, and no one listens to forbidden music. The Morality Police may admonish, fine, or arrest any violators, and those who are arrested will be tried in a Sharia court. Few will be able to prove their innocence.

The guilty may be imprisoned, flogged, suffer the amputation of a hand or foot, or be subjected to public execution. Are floggings, amputations, stonings, or beheadings cruel? Of course not! These punishments are intended only to promote virtue and prevent vice.

As citizens of the Islamic State of North America, there is no need to live in fear. The laws of the state are clear and perfectly reasonable. If a man is careful never to trim his beard, cut his hair inappropriately, or play cards, dominoes, or music, he has nothing to fear from the Morality Police. If a woman never steps outside without being fully covered, and if she makes sure never to pluck her eyebrows or wear cosmetics, she has no reason to be afraid. If children never steal, never play with forbidden Western-style toys, and never whisper or laugh during prayers, they never have to fear the Morality Police.

ISNA authorities have issued many flyers and pamphlets telling citizens of the Islamic State of North America how to speak, behave, think, dress, and pray just as the Prophet and his companions did fourteen centuries ago. Under the old US Constitution, the American people were oppressed by a wide array of freedoms that caused them to continually transgress the merciful rules and regulations set forth by the Prophet. But now, with the clarity of Sharia law, every man knows right to the centimeter the precise spot on his calf where his trousers should be hemmed—no lower, no higher. The people are blessed and happy because they know exactly what the state expects of them in even the smallest details of their lives.

Of course, only faithful Muslims enjoy these blessings. Christians, Jews, apostates, and idolaters face a much harsher existence. ISNA's Ministry of Collections and Distributions confiscates homes, cars, furnishings, and appliances from the infidels and redistributes them to the faithful. Families of Islamic martyrs never have to pay for housing, utilities, or other necessities of life because ISNA makes sure they are rewarded with worldly goods confiscated from the idolaters. And what better way to prove oneself worthy of receiving such blessings than by informing on one's neighbors to the Morality Police?

The Islamic State of North America uses all the latest

technology to turn back the clock of civilization to the seventh century AD. Computers, the Internet, smartphones, security cameras, and flying drones maintain constant surveillance and control of the people. The Islamic State uses high-speed computers to watch every person and listen in on every conversation, whether on the street, in the office, at the market, or in the so-called privacy of the home.

Every phone, every computer, and every TV is a listening device for the watchful eye of the Islamic State. There is no place to hide, no place where the state cannot watch, hear, and apprehend you. The Islamic State of North America will eliminate all sin and vice by making sure every citizen is monitored at all times. Nothing escapes the notice of the state.

Released from the oppression of free will, the people are happy and grateful subjects of the new Islamic utopia. At least, that's what the ISNA leaders say.

But will we prevent it?

It may seem as if the future I've just described is farfetched, impossible, and maybe even alarmist. But so many world-changing events—from even just the past few decades—seemed fanciful and unbelievable . . . until they happened.

Few so-called experts in foreign policy believed President Reagan's prediction that the Soviet Union would collapse—until he was proved right less than three years after leaving office. Investors failed to heed warnings about the dangers of deregulation, derivatives, and risky loans until the 2008 global financial crisis nearly plunged the world into another Great Depression. No one predicted the widespread surge of the Arab Spring that swept across North Africa and the Middle East from late 2010 to 2012. Likewise, the "experts" were caught off-guard by the results of the June 2016 Brexit referendum (in which British voters chose to pull out of the European Union). Many American "experts" were equally astonished by the November 2016 election victory of Donald Trump over a seemingly unbeatable Hillary Clinton.

Considering these "impossible" events that have already happened, can we really say with confidence that an Islamic State of North America could never happen?

In March 2018, a Muslim lawyer and scholar named Ahmed Abdou Maher published an Arabic-language article in an Egyptian publication. I discovered it on christian-dogma. com, an Arabic-language Christian website. The article is titled "Why Don't Christians and Jews Accept Our Islam?" If Mr. Maher had been writing to a Western audience, using the politically correct terms of our culture, he might have titled it "Why Are Christians and Jews So Islamophobic?" The article is a remarkably frank and honest examination of how Muslims have treated non-Muslims down through history and of the treatment we might expect under a future Islamic caliphate. Here is an excerpt, which I have translated from Arabic:

> How unjust our Muslim ancestors were to Allah and Islam when they invaded countries and looted the riches [of those countries] in the name of Islamic conquests—conquests that were not commanded by Islam or the Prophet of Islam [Muhammad]. . . .
>
> Imagine what [Muslim conquerors] offer you if you are a young [non-Muslim] man defending your country. If you were

captured, they would either kill you, sell you [into slavery], or you had better accept their Islam, which they impose on you.

And if you are a non-combatant civilian, they would give you two choices: (1) either you change your religion to become a Muslim overnight without even explaining to you what Islam is all about, or (2) you stay as you are but pay an oppressive *jizyah* [the tax of submission to Islam] while feeling humiliated and crushed.

Your daughters and children will be taken captive. And your wife will be a concubine to a bearded libertine who sleeps with her, saying that this is the ruling that Allah has revealed [in the Koran].

Your children will be their servants or a source of enjoyment for their desires. Or they may sell some of those they don't need in the slave market, convinced all the while that this shameful behavior is the rule of Allah.[6]

Maher goes on to explain in detail the kind of discrimination that non-Muslims must endure under Sharia law. For example, non-Muslims are not allowed to ride horses but are permitted to ride donkeys. They must ride without a saddle (only blankets are permitted), and riders may not straddle the donkey but may only ride with both legs dangling from one side.

A non-Muslim man cannot have a normal haircut; he must shave his head. In any gathering, non-Muslims cannot sit in the front rows but must sit in back. Non-Muslims may not lead meetings or councils.

Muslims may not greet non-Muslims with pleasantries, such as, "How are you?" or "How is your day?" Muslims are forbidden to give consolation to non-Muslims who are sick.

Non-Muslims may not walk in the middle of the road, but must walk close to the walls.

Non-Muslims may not build a new church or other building of worship, nor may they rebuild or repair ruined churches or buildings, even if those buildings were unjustly demolished. A non-Muslim may not build a structure higher than Muslim buildings. A non-Muslim is forbidden from publicly displaying wine, pork, a bell, or a Bible. A non-Muslim may not raise his or her voice during mourning, may not publicly display food or drink during the Muslim fasting month of Ramadan, and may not enter a mosque, even if invited to do so by a Muslim.

A non-Muslim may not enter a public restroom without wearing a ring of lead around his or her neck as a sign of submission. A Christian may not convert to Judaism or vice versa.

If a non-Muslim refuses to pay the jizyah tax and refuses to accept insult and humiliation from Muslims, his blood and money are to be wasted. Non-Muslims must stand in the presence of Muslims and are not to be honored among Muslims.

After listing these acts of discrimination and insult that Muslims show to non-Muslims, Ahmed Abdou Maher asks his fellow Muslims, "Would you deal with people in this brutal way to force them to become Muslims? . . . Would it be right to call all these actions the 'Sharia of Allah'? . . . Don't you see that the Koran doesn't call for any of these? . . . Don't then be surprised when others from all other religions hate you!"[7]

These are the words of a moderate Muslim scholar in Egypt, pleading with fellow Muslims to show respect for non-Muslims. But he is also painting a frightening word-picture for us of what life would be like for non-Muslims under an Islamic caliphate.

Where can your children, grandchildren, and great-grandchildren go to escape the iron grip of the Islamists? Not to Europe or Great Britain—those Western nations will undoubtedly fall to the Islamists before America ever does. If the Islamic State comes to power in the West, there will be no way to escape and nowhere to run. The Islamists will reign supreme, and their control will be absolute.

Welcome to your Islamic utopia.

2

A CENTURIES-OLD WAR

MOST AMERICANS BELIEVE that the war on terror began in late 2001, after the 9/11 attacks. But America's war with radical Islamic terrorism actually began more than two centuries ago, almost immediately after the United States became an independent nation.

With the signing of the Treaty of Paris between Great Britain and the United States, the Revolutionary War officially ended on September 3, 1783. One consequence of independence was that American merchant ships were no longer under the protection of the formidable British navy.

On October 11, 1784, as the American brigantine *Betsey* was bound from Spain to America with a cargo of salt, Moroccan pirates, all Muslims, boarded the vessel on the open seas and held the ten-man crew for ransom.

In the summer of 1785, Algerian pirates captured two US merchant ships, the *Dauphin* and *Maria*, and held twenty-one crew members and passengers hostage.

The Muslim pirates who terrorized the Mediterranean and eastern Atlantic were called Barbary corsairs (*corsair* is another word for *pirate*) because they came from four Muslim nations on the Barbary Coast of North Africa—the independent Sultanate of Morocco and three semi-autonomous provinces of the Ottoman Empire: Algiers (Algeria), Tunis (Tunisia), and Tripoli (Libya). The Barbary corsairs attacked vessels from predominantly Christian nations, capturing ships and cargos, and enslaving or ransoming the ships' passengers and crews. All four Barbary States extorted tribute (protection money) from the nations of Europe and America. A nation that wanted to navigate the seas in safety had to pay the Barbary racketeers in gold, jewels, guns, or ammunition. The Barbary pirates were engaged in what we now call state-sponsored terrorism.

In August 1786, three years before he was elected president, General George Washington lamented in a letter to his friend the Marquis de Lafayette, "In such an enlightened, in such a liberal age, how is it possible that the great maritime powers of Europe should submit to pay an annual tribute to the little piratical states of Barbary? Would to Heaven we had a navy able to reform those enemies to mankind, or crush them into non-existence."[1] In those early days of American history, the young nation not only lacked a navy, but it also lacked a constitution and a strong central government. As America struggled to get on its feet as a nation, it was incapable of responding to radical Islamic terrorism.

Historian Joseph Wheelan observes that the United States and the four Barbary States could not have been more different from each other. Where the United States was overwhelmingly Christian, the Barbary States were "solidly Moslem—and openly hostile toward Christians. The new American republic was a laboratory of Enlightenment ideals, especially freedom, openness, and rationality; the Barbary Powers were medieval, closed, tyrannical, and corrupt. . . . While America dreamed of global markets for its growing profusion of products, the Barbary rulers' narrow aims hadn't changed in centuries: to invoke the Koran to extort money from Christian nations."[2]

After the capture of the *Betsey*, *Dauphin*, and *Maria*, two top American diplomats—John Adams, ambassador to Great Britain, and Thomas Jefferson, ambassador to France—went to Europe to meet with ambassadors from the Barbary States, hoping to end the Islamist campaign of terror against American shipping. One evening in early 1786, Adams visited the London home of Ambassador Sidi Haji Abdrahaman of Tripoli. Abdrahaman invited Adams to sit with him by the fire and asked him many questions about life in America. The two men communicated in a mixture of Italian, French, and English. After a while, Abdrahaman said that America "is a very great country, but Tripoli is at war with it."[3]

Surprised, Adams asked the ambassador "how there could be war between two nations when there had been no hostility, injury, insult, or provocation on either side."[4] Abdrahaman replied that the Muslim nations along the Mediterranean were sovereigns of the sea. No nation could safely navigate there without making peace with Turkey, Tripoli, Tunis, Algiers, and Morocco. America could only purchase safety for its ships, the ambassador said, by paying tribute money to the Muslim nations.[5]

A few weeks later, Thomas Jefferson traveled to London from Paris, and Adams took him to meet Ambassador Abdrahaman. Again, Adams asked the ambassador from Tripoli what grounds the Barbary States claimed for making war against America.

The ambassador replied that the warlike policies of the Barbary States were, in Adams's words, "founded on the Laws of their Prophet, that it was written in their Koran, that all nations who should not have acknowledged their authority were sinners, that it was their right and duty to make war upon them wherever they could be found, and to make slaves of all they could take as Prisoners, and that every Musselman [Muslim] who should be slain in battle was sure to go to Paradise."[6]

Abdrahaman boasted that it was a law among the Barbary pirates that the crew and passengers of a captured ship would be divided among the pirates as slaves, and the first man to board an enemy ship would receive one more slave than his fellow pirates. As a pirate prepared to board an enemy ship, he would "take a dagger in each hand and another in his mouth, and leap on board, which so terrified their enemies that very few ever stood against them."[7]

Thomas Jefferson believed that the only answer to Islamic piracy and terrorism was war. He wanted America and Europe to join forces in blockading North Africa and putting an end to Barbary terrorism. But John Adams believed it was better to pay a high price in tribute than lose American lives in a distant war. "We ought not to fight them at all," Adams said, "unless we determine to fight them forever."[8]

The logic of jihad

As the young American nation struggled to pay the exorbitant tributes exacted by the Barbary States, the Islamists' demands kept going up, beyond what the government could afford. For a while, American ships took their chances navigating the Mediterranean and northeastern Atlantic. But by the end of 1793, Barbary pirates had seized a dozen ships from the United States, enslaving their passengers and crews under the vilest conditions imaginable.

Not content to limit their attacks to shipping, the Barbary pirates also raided coastal villages in Italy, France, Spain, and Portugal—and as far away as Britain and Ireland. Landing on unguarded beaches by night, they invaded homes by stealth and seized Christian men, women, and children to sell on the North African slave market.[9] In response, some European nations gave in to the Islamist demands for tribute, while others went to war against the Barbary pirates.

In March 1794, during George Washington's second term, Congress approved the construction of six naval vessels to protect American merchant ships at sea. When Washington signed the Naval Act into law, it established an American navy for the first time since the end of the Revolutionary War. However, a clause in the Naval Act stipulated that construction on US Navy ships would cease if a peace agreement was reached with Algiers—which happened early in 1796 before the ships were finished. Congress subsequently approved the completion of half the original order of ships, and those three vessels were launched in 1797.

When John Adams succeeded Washington as president, he authorized further tribute payments to Algiers in the form of cash, guns, and a thirty-six-gun warship. Moreover, he agreed to pay a ransom to the government of Algiers for the release of every American held prisoner—and the remains of thirty-seven sailors who had been worked or tortured to death in captivity. Unfortunately, this policy of appeasement made the problem of piracy and terrorism worse, not better. Though Adams was one of our founding fathers, and his intentions as president were noble, he didn't seem to appreciate the threat posed by Islamic terrorism.

Not surprisingly, American payments to Algiers emboldened other Barbary States to demand blackmail payments as well. When George Washington died in 1799, the pasha of Tripoli (Libya) told President Adams that it was a tradition in his culture that when a leader of a tributary state died, that state must send a gift to the pasha. A leader of Washington's stature, the pasha said, was worth a lavish gift in gold. President Adams paid it— and the demands of the Barbary States continued to grow more unreasonable year by year.

The most humiliating episode in John Adams's campaign of appeasement occurred in September 1800, when the US Navy warship *George Washington* sailed into the port of Algiers, laden with timber, fabric, and foodstuffs—the tribute the United States had agreed to pay. The commander of the *George Washington*, Captain William Bainbridge, was a war hero who had demonstrated gallantry in sea battles against the English and French. It galled him that his powerful warship, named for America's first president and greatest general, was used to deliver extortion payments to a bullying nation. Yet the first time a warship of the US Navy entered Mediterranean waters, it sailed on a disgraceful mission of appeasement.

After the *George Washington* anchored under the gun batteries of the Islamic fortress in Algiers, Captain Bainbridge went ashore to meet the *dey*—the regent who governed the province under authority of the Ottoman sultan at Constantinople. The dey inspected the cargo and declared that the tribute was insufficient—even though it met the agreed-upon price.

Eager to impress the Ottoman sultan by humiliating the Americans, the dey declared that the *George Washington* was now under the command of Algiers. He ordered Bainbridge to take down the American flag and replace it with the flag of Algiers, and then to deliver a shipment of African slaves, gold, lions, and other animals to the sultan in Constantinople. If Bainbridge refused, the dey told him he would order all the guns of the fortress to sink the *George Washington*. Captain Bainbridge had no choice but to obey.

American weakness in the face of Algerian bullying invited more extortion and terrorism from neighboring states. The pasha of Tripoli tripled his demand for payments from the US and added a requirement that an American gunmaker deliver guns ornamented with diamonds.

When Thomas Jefferson succeeded John Adams as president in March 1801, he was outraged that the US government was devoting nearly one-fifth of the national budget to pay tribute to the Barbary States. At the same time, the pasha of Tripoli was becoming impatient because the United States had not met his demands for greater tribute. He informed the American ambassador that Tripoli would multiply the demand for tribute by more than 2,000 percent—and if the United States refused to meet those demands, Tripoli would declare war on America. To underscore his threat, the pasha sent soldiers to chop down the flagpole at the American embassy.

One of Jefferson's first official acts as president was to stop the tribute payments and to punish the Barbary States for sponsoring terrorism. He sent the Navy and Marines to bombard pirate strongholds in the region we now know as Libya, Tunisia, and Algeria. Thus began the First Barbary War, which lasted from 1801 to 1805.

One famous American victory against the Barbary States was the Marines' assault on the city of Derna in Muslim-ruled Tripoli in 1805—the battle that inspired the famous line in "The Marines' Hymn" about "the shores of Tripoli." Marines also earned the nickname *leathernecks* during the First Barbary War, though the exact origin of the name is open to debate. One version of the story attributes the word *leatherneck* to the stiff leather collar—called a stock—worn by the Marines since the founding of the Corps as a separate branch of the military in 1798 to help them maintain an upright posture. Another version states that during the First Barbary War, Marines in battle discovered that the leather collar helped to deflect the blades of cutlasses—the short, curved swords used by the Muslim pirates. Many a brave Marine who might otherwise have been beheaded in battle was saved by his leatherneck stock.[10]

What ultimately shifted the balance of power in the Mediterranean was that, unlike Europe and America, the Barbary States showed no interest in developing the technologies of war.

While the Western nations built increasingly more sophisticated ships and weapons, the Islamist nations—which were primarily interested in extorting wealth from the Christian West—failed to modernize. Soon they became a weak, third-rate power in the region. With greater diligence on the parts of the American and European navies, the Barbary pirates ceased to be a threat, and the Barbary slave trade gradually came to an end.

Some historians suggest that the Barbary pirates shouldn't be compared to Islamist terrorists today because the pirates were not waging jihad (holy war) against America. The Barbary pirates, they claim, were merely self-interested criminals who happened to be Muslims and who murdered and plundered for profit.

But as Ambassador Abdrahaman told John Adams and Thomas Jefferson as far back as 1786, the policies of state-sponsored piracy were founded on the Koran, which (in the ambassador's view) gave the Barbary States the right and the duty to attack, rob, and enslave people from Christian nations. The Barbary pirates were undoubtedly motivated by greed, hatred, and bloodlust, but they were also devout Muslims who justified their actions according to the Koran. The passages of the Koran that, in their minds, justified acts of wanton piracy included the following:

> When your Lord revealed to the angels: I am with you, therefore make firm those who believe. I will cast terror into the hearts of those who disbelieve. Therefore strike off their heads and strike off every fingertip of them.
>
> KORAN 8:12 (MOHAMMAD HABIB SHAKIR TRANSLATION)

Fight those who do not believe in Allah, nor in the latter day, nor do they prohibit what Allah and His Messenger have prohibited, nor follow the religion of truth, out of those who have been given the Book, until they pay the tax in acknowledgment of superiority and they are in a state of subjection.

KORAN 9:29 (MOHAMMAD HABIB SHAKIR TRANSLATION)

The Muslim leaders of the Barbary States believed that tribute from Christian nations was their due. It was merely the tax of submission, jizya, that the Koran expects non-Muslims to pay as a sign of submission to the Muslim religion and Muslim culture.

Extreme, political Islam has been a foe of the West and America almost since our nation was founded. It is still a relentless foe of everything our civilization stands for today. But because many of our leaders have failed to learn the lessons of history, these are lessons we are doomed to repeat.

Throughout most of our history, Americans have felt invulnerable, insulated by two oceans from the troubles of the world. Even after September 11, 2001, we have given little thought to the possibility that Islamism might pose a genuine threat to our way of life. Few of us have tried to understand the Muslim worldview and how different it is from our own way of thinking. So once again, we in the West have been slow to realize that radical, political Islam has declared war on our civilization and is bent on our destruction.

3

AT WAR—AND UNAWARE

I WAS BORN IN EGYPT and raised in a Christian home, a third-generation Protestant. My ancestors were Coptic (which simply means Egyptian) Christians who endured persecution and held fast to their Christian faith amid the onslaught of Islam in the seventh century. Before the Muslim armies swarmed into Egypt from Arabia, Christians made up about 85 percent of the population. Today, there are about ten million Christians in Egypt, about one-tenth of the population, and most of them are Coptic Orthodox believers.

The reason Coptic Christians went from being the dominant majority to an oppressed minority in Egypt is that the Muslim invaders from Arabia were Islamists. In contrast to Christians, who share the Good News of their faith and invite people to receive Christ, the Islamists have always used a well-sharpened

sword to convert people to Islam. They came to the people of
Egypt and offered them a choice: either convert to Islam or be
executed. Christians and Jews (whom the Koran calls People
of the Book) were given a third option: They could choose to
keep their original faith by paying the jizya tax—which is really
a form of punishment for being a non-Muslim. Those who paid
the jizya were called *dhimmis*—that is, people under the "protection" of the Muslim state; but they were in fact second-class
citizens in a condition of servitude.

Many Coptic Christians in the seventh century refused to
compromise their faith, and those who could afford it paid the
tax. Others faced death rather than convert to Islam. So it's a
miracle that the lineage of my Coptic Christian ancestors continued for more than thirteen centuries under the oppression
of Islamic rule.

I spent my formative years as a Christian in the Islamic
Egyptian culture. Most of my school friends were Muslims,
and I have many Muslim friends to this day. I frequently travel
in the Middle East and often talk to Muslims there. I live with
one foot in the Christian West and one foot in the Islamic
East, and I want to be clear about this: There is a distinction
between Islam and Islamism, between moderate Muslims and
Islamists. Though all Islamists are Muslims, not all Muslims
are Islamists. In fact, I have many Muslim friends who are as
strongly opposed to the Islamists as we are in the West.

What is an Islamist? An Islamist is a person who believes
that Islamic principles should strictly govern public life and
political policy. Islamists are zealous to make Sharia law the
ultimate authority over every aspect of commerce, government,

and political life. The worldview of Islamists has many names, including Islamism, political Islam, and Islamic fundamentalism. As difficult as it may be for most Westerners to understand, an Islamist envisions the perfect utopian society as a world ruled by a theocratic totalitarian state governed by the principles of the Koran—a world so rigidly controlled, so lacking in human free will that sin and vice would be impossible. That's why the Western concept of human freedom is so despised by Islamists.

Lara Logan, the chief foreign affairs correspondent for CBS News and *60 Minutes*, has been reporting from war zones and trouble spots across the Islamic world since 2002. Having spent much of her career covering the wars in Afghanistan and Iraq, Logan reported from the thick of the Battle of Haifa Street in Baghdad in early 2007—though reports and video she sent back were so intense that CBS producers censored her coverage. While reporting from Tahrir Square during the Egyptian revolution in February 2011, Logan was sexually assaulted by Muslim revelers who shouted that she was a Jew. She thought she was about to die, but a group of Muslim women pulled her away from her attackers and led her to safety. After her return to the United States, she required multiple hospitalizations for her injuries and spoke candidly about the attack.

Lara Logan has seen the best and the worst of the Muslim world. She once told an interviewer, "Islamic terrorists and jihadists that I have met over the years have all corrected me when I have said that Islam is a religion. They all tell me that Islam is a civilization. It's not a religion. And that's part of our problem [in dealing with the Islamic world]. We look at it as a religion. . . . What a civilization does is it prescribes rules for every part of your life, so it's an instrument for enormous control."[1]

Some proponents of the Islamic faith claim that the word *Islam* is Arabic for *peace*. But even though *Islam* sounds similar to *salaam* (the Arabic word for *peace*), it actually means *submission* or *surrender*. Islam demands unconditional obedience from its followers.

In Christianity, we speak of surrendering our lives and hearts to Jesus Christ. But there is a vast difference between the surrender that Christ calls us to and the surrender that Islam demands. When we surrender to Christ, he sets us free. As Paul writes in Galatians 5:1, "It is for freedom that Christ has set us free. Stand firm, then, and do not let yourselves be burdened again by a yoke of slavery."

But when a person converts—surrenders—to Islam, he becomes a slave to a vast array of rules, regulations, and religious laws, which must be kept to the letter. A Muslim never knows if he has done enough, lived a pure enough life, given enough alms, and prayed fervently enough to please Allah. A Muslim can never be certain whether he is going to paradise or hell—unless he goes to his death by martyrdom. Islamists believe that martyrdom—dying in the defense of Islam—is the only guaranteed path to heaven, and that's why terrorist groups are able to recruit volunteers for suicide missions.

Christians who surrender to Jesus are eternally secure and free. Muslims who surrender to Islam are enslaved and uncertain about their eternal fate. Fundamentalist Islam demands that its followers work to bring the entire world into submission and surrender to Islam.

The Barbary pirates who captured and enslaved Europeans and Americans in the seventeenth and eighteenth centuries were carrying out the radical objective of their religion—making war on the non-Muslim world and seeking to force the "infidels" to submit and surrender. They attacked American and European ships with the same Islamist zeal shown by the nineteen hijackers on September 11, 2001.

The Islamist jihad is still being waged against the West today—sometimes through violence and terror and other times through stealth and infiltration. Though the Islamists have declared war against us, our leaders have often been unwilling to admit that we are at war.

A missed opportunity

During the 1990s in Sudan, the Mukhabarat (the Sudanese central intelligence agency) compiled thick files of information on a then little-known terrorist network called al-Qaeda and its Saudi Arabian founder, Osama bin Laden. According to David Rose of *Vanity Fair*, "the Sudanese government made numerous efforts to share this information with the United States—all of which were rebuffed. On several occasions, senior agents at the FBI wished to accept these offers but were apparently overruled by President Clinton's secretary of state, Madeleine Albright, and her assistant secretary for Africa, Susan Rice."[2]

Sudan was in an excellent position to keep tabs on bin Laden because the terrorist leader, his family, and his followers had been living there since early 1991. Bin Laden not only ran al-Qaeda from Sudan, but he also operated a construction company that was building infrastructure for Sudan—roads, agricultural projects, and an airport. Though the Sudanese had invited bin Laden into their country, they kept him and his entourage under close surveillance.

By early 1996, the Clinton administration became concerned about Osama bin Laden. Though bin Laden had not carried out attacks against American interests, he had waged a campaign of terror against US allies in the Middle East.

In March 1996, seeking an improved relationship with the United States, the government of Sudan sent its minister of defense, Major General Elfatih M. Erwa, to the US. He met with American officials at a hotel in Rosslyn, Virginia, outside of Washington, DC. The Americans told Erwa that, if Sudan wanted better relations with the US, the Sudanese government should provide information about Osama bin Laden. Erwa was prepared to do much more than provide information. He told the Americans that Sudan was ready to deliver bin Laden into US custody.

Janet McElligott, who had served in the first Bush Administration, acted as a go-between in talks between the FBI and the Sudanese intelligence service. She later reported, "Erwa offered to hand bin Laden to the United States on a silver platter . . . but the representatives of the United States told Erwa the United States only wanted bin Laden out of Sudan."[3]

On February 15, 2002, former president Bill Clinton gave a speech to the Long Island Association in New York. After his talk, he answered questions about terrorism (the 9/11 attacks had occurred five months earlier). "We tried to be quite aggressive with [terrorists]," he said. "Mr. bin Laden used to live in Sudan. He was expelled from Saudi Arabia in 1991, then he went to Sudan. And we'd been hearing that the Sudanese wanted America to start dealing with them again. . . . At the time, 1996, he had committed no crime against America, so I did not bring him here because we had no basis on which to hold him, though we knew he wanted to commit crimes against America."[4]

Sometime later, when President Clinton realized he had inadvertently admitted passing up an opportunity to prevent 9/11, he claimed he had misspoken. Elfatih Erwa was emphatic in stating that Sudan offered Osama bin Laden to the United States government in 1996 and that the Clinton administration rejected the offer, but the 9/11 Commission later concluded that "no credible evidence" of a Sudanese offer existed.[5] On the other hand, journalist Lawrence Wright, author of the Pulitzer Prize-winning book *The Looming Tower*, interviewed Erwa and studied the evidence, and he said "it seems clear that the director of national security at the time . . . did explore the possibility of accepting bin Laden."[6]

Whether the Sudanese offer happened or not, the threat that Osama bin Laden posed to the United States was well-known to our government by 1996. An al-Qaeda plot to blow up skyscrapers in New York City was uncovered in November 1990, and there were al-Qaeda connections to the 1993 World Trade Center truck bombing attack. By 1994, bin Laden had joined forces with the Egyptian Islamic Jihad, which staged a failed assassination attempt against Egyptian president Hosni Mubarak in 1995.

After Sudan expelled Osama bin Laden on May 18, 1996, he set up shop in the rugged mountains of Afghanistan. From there, on August 23, he issued a "Declaration of War Against the

Americans Who Occupy the Land of the Two Holy Mosques."
In March 1997, bin Laden told an interviewer for CNN, "We
declared jihad against the US government, because the US government is unjust, criminal, and tyrannical."[7]

On February 22, 1998, bin Laden issued a *fatwa* (a religious
edict) calling for attacks on all Americans, including civilians:

> We—with God's help—call on every Muslim who believes in
> God . . . to kill the Americans and plunder their money wherever
> and whenever they find it. . . . The ruling to kill the Americans
> and their allies—civilians and military—is an individual duty for
> every Muslim who can do it in any country in which it is possible
> to do it, in order to liberate the al-Aqsa Mosque and the holy
> mosque [in Mecca] from their grip, and in order for their armies
> to move out of all the lands of Islam, defeated and unable to
> threaten any Muslim.[8]

Osama bin Laden and al-Qaeda continued to plot their
attacks against American interests around the world. They were
at war with the United States, even if the United States was not
yet at war with them.

On August 7, 1998, truck bombs exploded simultaneously
at US embassies in two East African cities: Nairobi, Kenya, and
Dar es Salaam, Tanzania. The Nairobi blast killed 213 people
and wounded some four thousand others, and the Dar es Salaam
blast killed eleven and wounded eighty-five. In all, a dozen
Americans died, and the rest of the victims were Africans or citizens of other countries. These attacks were acts of war directed
by Osama bin Laden.

On October 12, 2000, in Aden harbor in Yemen, suicide bombers in a small fiberglass boat set off a massive explosion, blasting a hole in the port hull of the guided missile destroyer USS *Cole*. Seventeen US sailors died and thirty-nine were wounded. It was another act of war by Osama bin Laden and al-Qaeda—a war bin Laden had loudly and publicly declared.

Even after these attacks, America was *still* not at war with the Islamists. The American government saw these terrorists as criminals to be brought to justice, not as a serious threat to America. After all, the attacks occurred halfway around the world, in places few Americans could find on a map. Yes, it was tragic for those who died and for their families. Yes, this bin Laden character had declared jihad against the West and called for the killing of civilians—but it wasn't a *real* war, was it? These terrorists couldn't *really* strike at America, could they?

Then came 9/11—the twin towers burned and collapsed in lower Manhattan, and smoke rose above the Pentagon and from a field near Shanksville, Pennsylvania. Only then did we finally understand that we were at war.

Today, the War on Terror is well into its second decade, with no end in sight. Yet most Americans are only dimly aware that we are still fighting that war. Our news outlets rarely report on the Americans who are fighting and dying in Afghanistan, much less in places like Niger, Nigeria, Somalia, Syria, and other zones of the shadow war against Islamist terrorism.

Most Americans are even less aware of another form of jihad that is being waged against Western civilization. It's a "cultural jihad," a war of subversion and infiltration, a war that seeks to use our Western laws, our freedoms, and our compassion against us. The new cultural jihadists have forged alliances with the political Left to make inroads against Western society.

When Ambassador Abdrahaman told John Adams in 1786 that his Islamist nation of Tripoli was at war with America, Adams couldn't comprehend it. When Adams became president of the United States, he responded to the Barbary States' acts of war with appeasement, tribute, and ransom payments. When Osama bin Laden told the world that al-Qaeda was at war with America, the American government couldn't comprehend it and failed to take the threat seriously—until we all awoke to the horrors of 9/11.

We can better understand how the Third Jihad will be waged by examining the First and Second Jihads and how the Christian world responded. That is where we now turn our attention.

4

THE FIRST JIHAD

MUHAMMAD, THE FOUNDER OF ISLAM, was born in Mecca in AD 570. His father died before he was born, and his mother died when he was five, so Muhammad was raised by relatives. When he was twelve, his uncle, an Arab trader named Abu Talib, took him on a journey to Syria. Along the way, young Muhammad visited many towns around Palestine and listened to his uncle's conversations with Christians and Jews.

In later years, Muhammad heard Christian preachers and Jewish teachers who visited Mecca. Illiterate and unable to read the Jewish and Christian Scriptures for himself, he listened to and absorbed both information and misinformation about Christian and Jewish beliefs.

When he was twenty-five, Muhammad made a trip to Syria to talk to Syrian Christians and learn their ways and beliefs.

He emerged from his study with a tragically distorted view of Christian teachings, especially on the divinity of Jesus, the nature of the Trinity, and the role of Mary. He thought that Christians worshiped three gods—God the Father, Jesus the Son, and Mary. He thought that Christians held beliefs similar to those of Arab pagans who believed in many gods—gods that had sexual relations with human women and produced children known as "the sons of the gods."

Because Muhammad misunderstood the Christian doctrine of the Incarnation, he refused to believe that Jesus was born of God. He revered Jesus as a great prophet and teacher, but instead of calling Jesus the Son of God, he referred to him as the son of Mary.

Muhammad spent a great deal of time meditating in solitude in the hills near Mecca. A cave north of the city was his favorite place to think. His biographer, Ibn Ishaq, describes an encounter that Muhammad claimed to have had in the cave with the angel Gabriel, who was holding a rich silken cloth on which some words were written.

The angel commanded Muhammad, "Read."

"I cannot read it," Muhammad said, confessing his illiteracy.

The angel continued to command him: "Read. . . . Read in the name of the Lord thy creator, who created man from a drop of blood. Read, thy Lord is the most bountiful, who taught by means of the pen, taught man what he knew not."[1]

Muhammad left the cave and told his wife and neighbors that Allah had sent him out to preach to the people of Arabia. His wife became his first convert. A male slave of the household was his next. Then two of his friends, Abu Bakr and Umar ibn al-Khattab, began following him and listening to his teachings. (After Muhammad's death, Abu Bakr and Umar ibn al-Khattab succeeded him as leaders of the Muslim community.)

The people of Muhammad's own tribe in Mecca refused to acknowledge him as a prophet because they wanted to continue in their idol worship. Muhammad incorporated many Jewish traditions into his new religion, and some of the Jews living in and around Mecca developed a friendship with him.

From the time he was forty until his death at age sixty-three, Muhammad dictated the message of the Koran to several followers, who wrote down and compiled the message. Muslims believe that Allah revealed the message of the Koran to Muhammad through the angel Gabriel. The Koran contains some of the same stories found in the Bible, though with variations in details, including the story of Abraham, Hagar, and Ishmael, the destruction of Sodom and Gomorrah, and stories about Jacob and Joseph. Some stories in the Koran appear to be versions of ancient legends that had been told since before Muhammad was born.

After Muhammad's message was rejected in Mecca, he and his followers undertook a mass migration (called the Hegira) to the city of Yathrib (renamed Medina, or "City of the Prophet," after Muhammad's death). In Yathrib, Muhammad's message was widely received by both Arabs and Jews, and the various tribes of the city united under the banner of Muhammad's new religion. It's possible that the Jews in Medina were receptive to Muhammad's message because they lacked copies of their own Scriptures and couldn't detect the errors and discrepancies in his teachings.

Some of Muhammad's teachings seem designed to accommodate the traditions of his early Jewish followers. The Jewish day of atonement, Yom Kippur (the holiest day on the Hebrew calendar) became Ashura, the Islamic day of remembrance. In Mecca, Muhammad had called his followers to twice-daily prayers; in Medina, he increased that call to three times a day because the Jews prayed morning, noon, and night. He later increased it to five times a day, as Muslims observe today. The Muslims in Medina made Friday their holy day of the week.

The cordial relationship between Muslims and Jews could not last. The more clearly the Jews understood Muhammad's message, the more they realized that this new religion was at odds with the Hebrew Scriptures. As the Jews turned away from Muhammad's message, he angrily accused them of forsaking the truth. He and his followers began confiscating the property of the Jews and driving them away from Medina.

Muhammad's teachings changed over time, gradually becoming more extreme and militant. In the early days of his preaching, he called the pagans of the Arabian Peninsula to belief in Allah, whom he identified as the God of Abraham. In time, he began to equate his revelation with that of the Hebrew and Christian Scriptures, and he placed himself on an equal plane with Moses and Jesus (who are called Musa and Isa, respectively, in Islam). Ultimately, Muhammad proclaimed his message to be Allah's final revelation, superseding the Scriptures of both Judaism and Christianity. Islam, he claimed, was the faith that began with Abraham (the first Muslim, according to Muhammad). This new revelation, he said, was delivered in the Arabic language, and the Arabs would henceforth have a prophet and a holy book of their own.

During the first dozen years after his vision in the cave, Muhammad lived in Mecca and taught a religion that was primarily concerned with the inner struggle to live a righteous spiritual life. During those years, he attracted fewer than two hundred converts to his new religion.

But when Muhammad led his followers to Yathrib in 622, his message underwent a profound change, from one of inner struggle to an outward struggle against unbelievers. Islam became an aggressive, warlike religion—and Muhammad began to attract followers in droves. The number of Muslim followers quickly swelled to about ten thousand. Islam was no longer just a religion; it was an army—and Muhammad set out to conquer the world with his Islamic army, starting with the Arabian Peninsula.

Twenty years after founding the Muslim religion, Muhammad was stricken with a sudden fever and died. Before his death, he achieved his goal of founding a religion that controlled every aspect of its followers' daily lives—and he and his followers successfully unified most of Arabia under Muslim rule. He also set forth a vision of a world completely dominated by the Muslim religion. The goals of fundamentalist, political Islam remain the same as they were in Muhammad's lifetime: total control of every Muslim's entire life and the establishment of a theocratic world empire.

Wars of Islamic expansion

After Muhammad's death in 632, he was succeeded by his friend Abu Bakr, who took the title of *caliph*, the leader of the Muslim community. Abu Bakr led the armies of Islam in a campaign known as the Ridda wars (also called the Wars of Apostasy), which crushed the rebellion of tribes that rejected Abu Bakr as their caliph.

Next, Abu Bakr sent an Arab general, Khalid ibn al-Walid, to make war against the Sasanian Empire (modern-day Iran) and the Byzantine Empire in Syria. Khalid's successful campaigns were the beginning of Islam's First Jihad, the first campaign to spread Islamic rule beyond the borders of Arabia.

Abu Bakr is also credited by Sunni Muslims with ordering that the Koran be compiled and preserved in its present written form. He reigned as the first caliph for two years, two months, and two weeks—a reign that ended with his illness and death.

Abu Bakr was succeeded by the second caliph, Umar ibn al-Khattab, Muhammad's other close friend and follower. Umar expanded Abu's campaign of jihad, leading the Muslim armies into Persia (present-day Iran), central Asia, and the Punjab region of modern-day Pakistan and India. The warlike and imperialist actions of early Islam were motivated by passages in the Koran such as this:

> Fight those who do not believe in Allah, nor in the latter day, nor do they prohibit what Allah and His Messenger have prohibited, nor follow the religion of truth, out of those who have been given the Book, until they pay the tax [the jizya religious tax] in acknowledgment of superiority and they are in a state of subjection.
>
> And the Jews say: Uzair [Ezra] is the son of Allah; and the Christians say: The Messiah [Christ] is the son of Allah; these

are the words of their mouths; they imitate the saying of those
who disbelieved before; may Allah destroy them; how they are
turned away!

KORAN 9:29-30 (MOHAMMAD HABIB SHAKIR TRANSLATION)

Early Islam was the same brand of radical, political, fundamentalist Islam we see in Islamist groups such as al-Qaeda,
ISIS, and the Muslim Brotherhood today. They believe that
Allah commands all Muslims to subjugate the adherents of
every rival religion, especially Jews and Christians, and to conquer their lands.

The Koran's call for Muslims to subjugate non-Muslim people
and dominate the world in the name of Allah is a counterfeit
commission, a false substitute for the Great Commission, the
Lord's command that Christians are to win the world for Christ
by preaching a gospel of peace. Christians are called by God to
conquer the world—not by the sword, not by subversion and
subterfuge, but by spreading God's message of grace and truth.
Jesus sent his followers into the world to preach the Good News
and invite all people to accept Jesus as Lord and Savior: "Go
into all the world and preach the gospel to all creation. Whoever
believes and is baptized will be saved, but whoever does not
believe will be condemned."[2]

Jesus told Pontius Pilate, "My kingdom is not of this world.
If it were, my servants would fight to prevent my arrest by the
Jewish leaders. But now my kingdom is from another place."[3]
The kingdoms of this world are kingdoms of the sword. The
Kingdom of Jesus is not of this world. It advances by attrac-
tion, not compulsion. Christianity always invites, never forces.

Those who freely accept Jesus as Lord by faith will be saved. Those who reject the Good News will perish in eternity—but they are free to make that choice. They will not be forced into submission at the point of a sword.

It's astonishing how rapidly the Muslim armies conquered distant lands during Islam's first century. One historical reason for Islam's many battlefield successes was the weakness of their enemies. The Byzantine-Sasanian wars of the sixth and seventh centuries had exhausted two once-great empires: the Eastern Roman (Byzantine) Empire and the Sasanian (Neo-Persian) Empire. (The Western Roman Empire had fallen in the fifth century.) After decades of war, neither empire had the economic or military strength to mount a defense against the motivated Muslim armies.

A second historical reason for Islam's early success was the Plague of Justinian, a pandemic that raged through the Byzantine and Sasanian empires in the sixth century, killing an estimated 25 million people during its initial outbreak. The plague, named for the Eastern Roman emperor Justinian I, who contracted and survived the disease, was a bubonic bacterial disease that later became known as the Black Death. The combination of war and plague paved the way for the rise of militant Islam and the uncanny success of the First Jihad.

The eight conquests of the First Jihad

The First Jihad began during the lifetime and under the leadership of Muhammad himself. It began around 622, continued after Muhammad's death in 632, and lasted for almost 130 years, until 751. In that relatively short span of history, Islam grew from a handful of followers in Mecca to a religious empire stretching from the Atlantic shores of Europe and Africa to the western borders of China. The First Jihad consisted of eight conquests in eight regions of the world.

The first conquest was of the Levant, a region encompassing modern-day Israel, Lebanon, Jordan, and Syria. The conquest of the Levant began in 634 and was completed by 641. News of the Ridda wars in Arabia prompted the Byzantine Empire to send an expeditionary force into southern Palestine. The Byzantine forces met the army of Khalid ibn al-Walid at the Battle of Ajnadayn, and the Arab army decimated the Byzantines. Over the next few years, Khalid's armies conquered the great fortified cities of the Levant, including Damascus in 636, Jerusalem in 638, and Caesarea in 640—important cities in Christian history.

The second conquest of the First Jihad was Egypt, from 639 to 642. At that time, Egypt was a strategically vital Byzantine province because of its Mediterranean seaports and grain exports. Egypt was also culturally vital because of its long history as a great power under the Pharaohs, its many Christian churches at that time, and the Great Library of Alexandria, the repository of nearly all the written knowledge of the known world.

Egypt had been a majority Christian nation since Roman times, having been evangelized by Mark, the author of the Gospel of Mark, around AD 33. Today's Coptic Church in Egypt is directly descended from the churches first planted by Mark. The early church fathers Origen and Clement of Alexandria wrote, preached, and debated their opponents in the city of Alexandria.

The second caliph, Umar ibn al-Khattab, sent General Amr ibn al-As into Egypt to conquer the land for Allah. The Muslim army defeated the Byzantine forces at the Battle of Heliopolis in 640. That victory opened the door to the Islamic conquest of the entire province.

The great city of Alexandria fell to General Amr in 642. When the city surrendered, Amr sent a messenger to Umar, asking for instructions regarding the Great Library and its countless thousands of irreplaceable scrolls. These were books on history, science, mathematics, and religion as well as ancient works of drama and fiction. The messenger returned with instructions from the caliph: "If the writings of the Greeks agree with the Koran, they are superfluous and need not be preserved; if they disagree, they are pernicious and ought not to be preserved."[4] Tragically, General Amr ordered all the precious human knowledge of the ages to be fed to the furnaces as fuel. History records that it took six months to incinerate the entire collection of the Great Library of Alexandria.

Historian Hugh Kennedy observes, "Of all the early Muslim conquests, that of Egypt was the swiftest and most complete. Within a space of two years, the country had come entirely under Arab rule. Even more remarkably, it has remained under Muslim rule ever since. Seldom in history can so massive a political change have happened so swiftly and been so long lasting."[5]

The third conquest of the First Jihad was the Muslim conquest of Mesopotamia and Persia between 633 and 651. Though the Persian army of King Yazdgerd III was militarily weak, the mountainous terrain and fortifications of the ancient

Persian strongholds slowed the Muslim armies. It took nearly two decades for the Muslim forces to win a final victory over the Persians.

The fourth conquest of the First Jihad was the conquest of Sindh, the Indian subcontinent, from 711 to 714.

The fifth conquest of the First Jihad, the Muslim defeat of the Maghreb (Byzantine North Africa), took nearly a hundred years to complete, from 647 to 742. The conquest of the Maghreb began soon after Egypt had been secured. In 670, Muslim armies established a settlement at Qayrawan, in modern-day Tunisia, which became their forward-operating base. From Qayrawan, the Muslim armies moved out to capture Carthage in 698 and Tangiers by 708.

The sixth conquest of the First Jihad was the Muslim conquest of the Iberian Peninsula (modern Spain and Portugal) and the invasion of Gaul (modern France), from 711 to 721. Once the Muslim armies had secured Tangiers, a Moroccan city at the western entrance of the Strait of Gibraltar, the invasion force was separated from Spain by only nine miles of water. The commander of the Muslim army was Tariq ibn Ziyad (for whom the Rock of Gibraltar is named—Gibraltar comes from the Arabic *Jabal Tariq*, or "Mountain of Tariq"). The Iberian Peninsula was ruled by a Visigoth king named Roderic, often called the Last King of the Goths.

According to legend, a Visigoth nobleman named Don Julian, who commanded the fortress of Cueta, a short distance from Tangiers, sent his daughter to the palace of King Roderic to be educated. However, Roderic was a wicked and corrupt ruler, and he forced himself on the daughter. When news of this assault reached Don Julian, he sought revenge against the Visigoth king by colluding with Tariq ibn Ziyad to aid the Muslim invasion of Spain. Don Julian owned several merchant ships, which were anchored in the harbor at Ceuta. With these ships, he ferried seven thousand Muslim horsemen from Morocco to the Spanish shore at Gibraltar.

Though Roderic's forces heavily outnumbered the army of Tariq ibn Ziyad, the Muslim warriors swept across the Spanish mainland, capturing city after city. King Roderic was defeated and killed by Tariq's forces on July 19, 711, at the Battle of Guadalete, and Roderic's widow became the wife of the Muslim governor of Hispania.

By 713, the armies of Tariq ibn Ziyad had brought the entire Iberian Peninsula under Muslim control. The armies of Islam then turned east, moving into Gaul, with the intent to conquer all of Europe.

The seventh conquest of the First Jihad was the Muslim conquest of Transoxiana in central Asia—a region roughly equivalent to modern-day Uzbekistan, Tajikistan, and southern Kazakhstan—from 673 to 751.

The eighth conquest of the First Jihad was the Muslim conquest of modern Afghanistan (consisting of two Neo-Persian provinces called Khorasan and Sistan). The invasion of Afghanistan began with a Muslim victory over the Sasanian (Neo-Persian) forces of King Yazdgerd III in the Battle of Nahavand (which Muslims call the Victory of Victories). The defeat of Yazdgerd emboldened the province of Khorasan to revolt against Sasanian rule, opening the door to Muslim conquest of the region. Even after the Muslim armies gained control of the region, there were frequent uprisings and pockets of resistance for the next two centuries.

Shockwaves from the past

The wars that began with the conquest of the Arabian Peninsula during Muhammad's lifetime produced an Islamic caliphate stretching westward to Morocco and Portugal and eastward to India, touching the borders of China. This period of rapid conquest and expansion took place in the span of one century, resulting in the largest empire in history up to that time. The size of the Islamic caliphate was estimated at about five million square miles.[6]

As historian Edward Gibbon records in *The History of the Decline and Fall of the Roman Empire,* "The Arabian empire extended two hundred days' journey from east to west, from the confines of Tartary and India to the shores of the Atlantic Ocean. . . . The language and laws of the Koran were studied with equal devotion at Samarcand and Seville: the Moor and the Indian embraced as countrymen and brothers in the pilgrimage of Mecca; and the Arabian language was adopted as the popular idiom in all the provinces to the westward of the Tigris."[7]

The wars fought by Muhammad and his followers in the seventh and eighth centuries continue to send shockwaves into our own time and our own culture. Millions have died in the holy wars of jihad. Countless people have died in terror attacks around the world. The nation of Israel has been hemmed in by enemies and threatened with extinction. Around the world, Islamists call for the death of America and Western civilization.

Why?

It all comes down to one man and a vision he had in a desert cave in Arabia, fourteen centuries ago.

5

A DISASTROUS RESPONSE

THE CHRISTIAN CHURCH we read about in the book of Acts was a fellowship of believers who met in homes and preached the Good News in the synagogues and marketplaces. The early believers were poor and persecuted, yet they were eager to share the Good News of Jesus and bring more people into his Kingdom.

By the time of the First Jihad, the church had become institutionalized and powerful. The Christians of the first century would hardly have recognized the church of the seventh century. We look back on that time today and call it the Middle Ages or the Dark Ages. Though Jesus had once told Pontius Pilate, "My kingdom is not of this world," the institutional church of the Middle Ages was very much a kingdom of worldly power.

So, when the worldly kingdom of political Islam waged

its violent jihad against Christian lands, the worldly kingdom of the Latin Church responded by waging violent religious wars against its Islamic adversaries. These church-sanctioned wars eventually became known as the Crusades. Most of the Crusades involved military campaigns intent on recovering the Holy Land from Muslim occupation.

Even before the First Crusade was launched in 1096, the medieval church embarked on a military quest to recapture Spain and Portugal from Muslim rule—a quest known as the Reconquista (the Reconquest). The Ummayyad Islamic caliphate had subjugated the Iberian Peninsula by around 711. Though the Islamists had conquered Christian land, they could not conquer Christian hearts.

In 722, a small force of about three hundred men, led by a Christian Visigoth leader named Pelagius, defied Ummayyad demands that they surrender. The Ummayyad army, commanded by an Islamic general named Al Qama, vastly outnumbered the forces of Pelagius. The small Christian army, however, held the high ground in the mountains of Asturias. When Al Qama sent his battled-hardened troops into a valley to fight the Christians, a force of Christian soldiers was there to greet them, raining stones and arrows on the Ummayyad army from the rocks and cliffs above.

When Al Qama and his men turned back, they found their retreat cut off by Pelagius and the rest of his men, who had emerged from a hidden cave. In the ensuing battle, many Ummayyad warriors were killed, including General Al Qama. The rest of the Ummayyad army fled in panic. The cave in which Pelagius and his men hid before the battle became known as Covadonga (Cave of Worship), and the battle was commemorated as the Battle of Covadonga. After the battle, Pelagius was hailed as the ruler of the kingdom of Asturias. Islamic armies made many attempts to recapture Asturias but without success.

This victory by a small Christian army against a much larger Islamic army inspired many other Christians throughout Iberia to resist Muslim rule. The Reconquista continued century after century, reaching a major turning point in 1085 when Prince Alfonso VI of León and Castile recaptured Toledo. The Reconquista was completed by late 1248 when King Ferdinand III of León and Castile recaptured Seville in southern Spain.

The People's Crusade

In November 1095, Pope Urban II delivered a homily at the Council of Clermont in France, calling for volunteers to go to Palestine and make the land safe for Christians taking pilgrimages to the Holy Land. In his remarks, the pope promised the soldiers a works-based salvation that clearly violates the plan of salvation described in God's Word.

> All who die by the way, whether by land or by sea, or in battle against the pagans, shall have immediate remission of sins. This I grant them through the power of God with which I am invested. O what a disgrace if such a despised and base race, which worships demons, should conquer a people which has the faith of omnipotent God and is made glorious with the name of Christ! . . . Let those who, for a long time, have been robbers, now become knights. Let those who have been fighting against their brothers and relatives now fight in a proper way against the

barbarians. Let those who have been serving as mercenaries for small pay now obtain the eternal reward.[1]

In fact, Pope Urban made the same false promise to medieval Christians that the Koran makes to Muslims: *If you die as a martyr in a holy war, your sins will be forgiven.* Nowhere does the Bible make such a claim. The pope simply made up a doctrine and proclaimed it. Because of that promise, volunteers lined up to take their vows as Crusaders, receive an indulgence from the Church, and set off to reclaim Jerusalem for Christ. Some Crusaders even believed that, once they reached Jerusalem, a mass ascension would take place, and hundreds or thousands of Christian warriors would be taken up into heaven.

Even before this "officially sanctioned" First Crusade, a movement sprang up in Europe that became known as the People's Crusade or the Peasants' Crusade. But instead of being authorized by Pope Urban II or the church hierarchy, it was a popular expedition instigated by a smooth-talking monk from Amiens, France, known as Peter the Hermit. Peter dressed simply, rode a donkey wherever he went, and was famed for his ability to whip up a mob with his powerful oratory. He claimed that Jesus himself had appointed him to preach and lead a crusade against the nonbelievers. Judging from the results of his preaching, he was clearly the kind of false teacher the Bible warns us against.

The People's Crusade lasted from April to October in 1096 and left a trail of horrible atrocities in its wake. This self-appointed mob of ragtag crusaders carried out pogroms against defenseless Jews along the Rhine and Danube rivers, slaughtering innocent men, women, and children. Some Jews were forced at sword point to "convert" to Christianity. In most towns, the civil authorities and bishops tried to stop the violence and shield the Jews from harm, but they were unable to reason with the mobs. Historian Edward H. Flannery describes the carnage in *The Anguish of the Jews*:

> The massacres were clearly mob actions, reinforced by religious fanaticism. . . . Up to 10,000 [Jews] died, probably one fourth to one third of the Jewish population of Germany and Northern France at that time.
>
> The massacres left a stunned Jewish population and, as the accounts of various chroniclers show, a troubled Christian conscience. . . . [When the Holy Roman Emperor] Henry IV (1056–1106) returned from Italy and learned of the massacres, he punished whatever culprits he could find and permitted the forcibly baptized Jews to return to their former faith. . . . The harrowing experience left a deep scar on the Jewish psyche, especially in Germany. . . . Christians were viewed by some as capricious assassins, ever ready to strike.[2]

The mob passed through Germany and into Hungary, often pillaging houses and markets for food. They looted and burned the city of Belgrade and killed many Hungarians. They reached Constantinople, the Byzantine capital, and Peter the Hermit met with the Byzantine emperor, Alexius I Comnenus, telling him the People's Crusade was going to Asia Minor (Turkey) to make war against the Islamic armies there. Alexius warned against going to war with the Muslim Turks, but Peter and his mob wouldn't listen.

On the morning of October 21, 1096, Peter's untrained army of twenty thousand zealous foot soldiers marched toward Nicaea in northern Turkey—a Muslim stronghold that had once been rich in Christian history, the site of the first and second councils of Nicaea, and the place where the Nicene Creed was adopted. As the crusaders passed through a narrow valley with woods on either side, the sky was darkened as thousands of arrows rained down from Islamic archers, followed by an attack by Turkish soldiers on horseback. Seized with panic, the mob of crusaders was quickly routed, and most were slaughtered. Thus ended the infamous People's Crusade.

The First Crusade

Meanwhile, Pope Urban II authorized the first Crusade officially sanctioned by the church. The Crusaders began their journey on August 15, 1096, with about five thousand horse-mounted knights and thirty thousand foot-soldiers. Along the journey, hunger, disease, defection, and battles dramatically shrank their numbers. When the First Crusade reached the gates of Jerusalem on June 7, 1099, only fifteen hundred knights and twelve thousand foot-soldiers remained.

Many battle-hardened warriors wept openly upon seeing the Holy City for the first time. They quickly surrounded Jerusalem and laid siege. During the siege, Peter the Hermit—the French monk who had instigated, led, and survived the ill-fated People's Crusade—went around to the Valley of Jehoshaphat, the Garden of Gethsemane, and the Mount of Olives, preaching to the warriors and stirring them up for battle.

Jerusalem was occupied by the Fatimids, an Arabic Shia

Islamic caliphate that had captured the city the previous year from the Seljuks, a Turkish Sunni Muslim dynasty. Tens of thousands of Jews and Muslims huddled inside the city walls, awaiting the Crusaders' attack.

On the night of July 14, five weeks after their arrival at Jerusalem, the Crusaders launched two simultaneous assaults on the city's walls—rolling up wooden siege towers and raising wooden ladders to enable the warriors to scale the walls. The Islamic forces responded with pots of boiling oil and flaming arrows. Eventually, the Crusaders crashed the city gates with battering rams, forcing their way into the city. There they systematically slaughtered everyone in their path—soldiers and civilians, Muslims and Jews, men, women, and children. Historian Michael Hull describes the horrors and hot-blooded murder the Crusaders inflicted in the name of the Prince of Peace:

> The Crusaders spent at least that night and the next day killing Muslims, including all of those in the al-Aqsa Mosque. . . . Not even women and children were spared. The city's Jews sought refuge in their synagogue, only to be burned alive within it by the Crusaders. . . . The Europeans also destroyed the monuments to Orthodox Christian saints and the tomb of Abraham.
>
> There were no recorded instances of rape. The massacre was not insanity but policy, as stated by Fulcher of Chartres [a Crusader priest and eyewitness]: "They desired that this place, so long contaminated by the superstition of the pagan inhabitants, should be cleansed from their contagion." The Crusaders intended Jerusalem to be a Christian city—and strictly a Latin Christian city.[3]

Raymond of Aguilers, a Crusader chaplain, was an eyewitness to the carnage of that night. He recalled:

> Some of our men—actually, the more merciful ones—cut off the heads of their enemies. Others shot them with arrows, so that they fell from the towers. Others tortured them longer by casting them into the flames. Piles of heads, hands, and feet were to be seen in the streets of the city. One had to pick one's way over the bodies of men and horses. But these were small matters compared to what happened at the Temple of Solomon. You would not believe it if I told you. Suffice to say that in the Temple and porch of Solomon men rode in blood up to their knees and bridle reins. Indeed, it was a just and splendid judgment of God that this place should be filled with the blood of the unbelievers, since it had suffered so long from their blasphemies. The city was filled with corpses and blood.[4]

Does this account break your heart? It breaks mine! And I believe the Lord himself wept over Jerusalem as these horrible atrocities were committed in his name by warriors whose armor was emblazoned with the sign of the cross. There is no justification or excuse for the slaughter committed by the Crusaders in the conquest of Jerusalem. The bloody Crusader conquest of Jerusalem utterly violated the teachings of Jesus, the message of the gospel, and the character of God.

It should be acknowledged that many atheists, secularists, and other opponents of Judeo-Christian faith like to point to the Old Testament conquest of Canaan as evidence that the God of the Bible is a bloodthirsty, genocidal deity. But let's be clear: The God of the Old Testament is the same God as the God of the New Testament. He is a God who never changes, a merciful and compassionate God. Yet it is true that he ordered the Israelites to conquer Canaan, destroy Jericho and other cities, and slaughter their entire populations.

Any bloodshed is horrifying, but we need to understand *why* God ordered such wholesale slaughter. Sometimes, war becomes a necessary last resort for vanquishing evil and protecting the innocent.

Archaeologists have found evidence that the Canaanite tribes would sacrifice their children to the local deities by casting them to a fiery death in the furnace-like bellies of their idols. Some tribes placed their children in jars and suffocated them as sacrifices to their gods.

Before sending the Israelites into the Promised Land, God warned them to avoid the practices of the Canaanites: "You must not worship the LORD your God in their way, because in worshiping their gods, they do all kinds of detestable things the LORD hates. They even burn their sons and daughters in the fire as sacrifices to their gods."[5] So, when God commanded the Israelites to destroy the Canaanite tribes, it was not out of genocidal cruelty, but to extinguish their evil and bloody religious rites.

There's simply no comparison between God's righteous judgment of the Canaanites and the killing of Muslims and Jews during the Crusades. Jesus never called his church to slaughter unbelievers because their "superstition" was a "contagion." He never called his church to send people to hell, but to draw them into the Kingdom of Heaven. The crimes of the Crusades are a stain upon the honor of the Lord's church.

The Crusaders slaughtered many Muslims and Jews, though they also allowed some to live—but the defeated survivors were forced to leave the city with nothing. The Crusaders founded a government under the authority of the Roman Catholic Church, which they called the Kingdom of Jerusalem. They converted the Dome of the Rock mosque into a church. The Kingdom of Jerusalem lasted eighty-eight years, until Saladin, the first sultan of Egypt and Syria and the founder of the Sunni Ayyubid Dynasty, conquered Jerusalem in 1187. The Holy City remained in Muslim hands until the collapse of the Ottoman Empire after World War I.

A godly answer to the Crusades

In 1219, at the height of the Crusades, Francis of Assisi journeyed to Egypt to evangelize the sultan. Outside the walled port city of Damietta, he found a band of Crusaders camped around the city, more than a year into a long siege of the town. The people of Damietta were out of food and out of hope. Francis had compassion for the besieged Muslims, and he asked the Crusaders to show mercy to the people. The Crusaders refused.

Francis then went upstream along the Nile until he came to the camp of the sultan of Egypt, Malik al-Kamil, a nephew of Saladin's. When Sultan al-Kamil heard that the famed Italian friar had come to meet with him, he set a trap. He instructed his servants to spread out a carpet on the floor in front of his divan—a carpet decorated with Christian crosses. If Francis walked onto the carpet, the sultan reasoned, he could accuse Francis of insulting his own God. If Francis refused to walk on the carpet, he could accuse Francis of insulting the sultan himself.

When Francis arrived to meet the sultan, he strode boldly onto the carpet. The sultan sneered at him for treading the cross underfoot. But Francis replied, "Our Lord was crucified between two thieves. We Christians have the True Cross [of Christ]. The crosses of the thieves we have left to you, and I am not ashamed to tread on those."[6]

The sultan agreed to hear what the Christian missionary had come to say. So Francis preached the gospel of peace, the gospel of Jesus Christ, to Sultan Malik al-Kamil and his councillors and advisers. There is no evidence that any of the Muslim leaders in the sultan's court were moved to receive Jesus Christ as their Lord and Savior. But Francis of Assisi bore witness to them of God's grace and love—just as he bears witness to you and me of the way we should graciously, lovingly share Christ with the Muslims in our midst.

Later, Francis set forth rules that the brothers of his order should follow whenever they would go among the Muslims. He stressed that they must live humble and peaceful Christlike lives as a witness to the Muslims. They must avoid quarrels and disputes. They must "be subject" to the Muslims—in other words, defer to them, respect them, and speak humbly to them, not arrogantly or condescendingly.

Francis also quoted the words of Jesus from Matthew 10:16, that Christian missionaries are to be as shrewd as snakes but innocent as doves among enemies and unbelievers. They should "proclaim the word of God when they see it pleases God in order that (the unbelievers) might believe in God the almighty

Father and the Son and the Holy Spirit."[7] In other words, a Christian should be sensitive to the Spirit's leading and should not preach the gospel merely to provoke a confrontation or persecution.

Of course, any Christian missionary who preaches Christ in Muslim-occupied lands takes a considerable risk. "All the brothers, wherever they are," writes Francis, "should remember that they have given themselves and have abandoned their bodies to the Lord Jesus Christ. And for his love they must expose it to enemies, whether visible or invisible, for the Lord says: 'Whoever loses his life for my sake will save it (Matthew 16:25) for eternal life.'"[8]

We cannot defend the torture and mass slaughter committed by the Crusaders in the Middle Ages. In the name of Jesus, these misguided fanatics robbed and massacred both Muslims and Jews. There were a few wise and godly leaders of the church who, like Francis of Assisi, offered a godly answer to the Crusades and argued for a more Christlike approach to the Muslim world. One of these godly leaders was Roger Bacon, the thirteenth-century Oxford philosopher (and a friar of the order founded by Francis). Bacon warned that the Crusades were setting back the cause of Christ and his gospel because "those who survive, together with their children, are more and more embittered against the Christian faith."[9]

Enemies of the Christian faith like to cite the Crusades as evidence that Christianity is evil, hateful, murderous, and worthy of being suppressed or banned. Biologist Richard Dawkins, a leading popularizer of atheism, says it should be illegal for Christian parents to teach their faith to their children.[10] And he sees little difference between the jihad of Islam and the fanatical and murderous excesses of the Crusades. In *The God Delusion*, he writes:

> Muhammad and his followers . . . founded Islam upon a new holy book, the Koran or Qur'an, adding a powerful ideology of military conquest to spread the faith. Christianity, too, was spread by the sword, wielded first by Roman hands after the Emperor Constantine raised it from eccentric cult to official religion, then by the Crusaders.[11]

The obvious difference between Islam and Christianity, between the Islamist jihads and the Crusades of the Middle Ages, is that jihad is the literal fulfillment of commands written in the Koran. The torture and mass murder of the Crusades were a direct violation of the spirit and letter of the entire New Testament. Nowhere do we find Jesus or his apostles urging Christians to torture or kill in his name. Throughout the New Testament, we are enjoined to be peacemakers, to love one another and our enemies, to bless those who seek to harm us, and to share the good news of Jesus Christ as a gospel of peace and forgiveness, not war and condemnation.

Whenever people talk about the evils of the Crusades, they almost always leave out the fact that the Crusades were a belated reaction to more than four centuries of Islamic invasion, mass murder, forced conversion, and conquest of peaceful Christian lands. By the time the Crusades were proposed by Pope Urban II in the late eleventh century, Islam had subjugated half of Christendom by force—and without any retaliation from Christians. By that time, Muslim armies occupied cities that had once cradled the early church, including Antioch, Damascus, and Jerusalem in the Middle East, and Carthage, Hippo, and Alexandria in North Africa. Muslim armies had destroyed thousands of churches or turned them into mosques. Historian Robert Louis Wilken explains:

> By the middle of the eighth century more than fifty percent
> of the Christian world had fallen under Muslim rule. . . . The
> successors of Muhammad planted a permanent political and
> religious rival to Christianity and made Christians a minority in
> lands that had been Christian for centuries. Four hundred years
> later, when the Crusaders arrived in the East, an Arab historian
> observed that they had entered "the lands of Islam."[12]

The Crusaders entered the fray (originally, at least) to protect defenseless Christians from massacre and forced conversion by Muslim invaders. Still, the Muslim world has neither forgotten nor forgiven the murderous excesses of the Crusades. To this day, Islamists refer to Christians, Americans, and Westerners in general as Crusaders.

When you talk with Muslims or atheists about Christ, when you share the gospel with them, there's a chance they'll respond, "What about the Crusades? What about the murder and torture committed by people who followed the same Jesus you're preaching to me?" I don't want you to be blindsided by such questions. I want you to know the history of the First Jihad and the history of the Crusades. I want you to be able to respond to them with both grace and truth. I hope you'll follow the example set by Francis of Assisi and that you will bear a bold and uncompromising witness among your Muslim neighbors to God's deep grace and compassion for the Muslim world.

6

THE SECOND JIHAD

THE FIRST JIHAD BEGAN with Muhammad's vision in a cave in Arabia. The Second Jihad began with a vision that a Turkish warrior received in a dream.

The warrior was Osman I, about whom very little is known. According to tradition, Osman was asleep in the house of a Muslim holy man named Sheikh Edebali. The fifteenth-century Ottoman historian Aşıkpaşazâde describes the dream in *The Chronicles of the House of Osman*, written a century and a half after Osman's death:

> He [Osman] saw that a moon arose from the holy man's breast
> and came to sink in [his own] breast. A tree then sprouted from
> his navel, and its shade compassed the world. Beneath this shade
> there were mountains, and streams flowed forth from the foot of

each mountain. Some people drank from these running waters, others watered gardens, while yet others caused fountains to flow. When Osman awoke he went and told the story to the sheykh [holy man], who said, "Osman, my son, congratulations, for God [Allah] has given the imperial office to you and your descendants, and my daughter Malkhun shall be your wife."[1]

Many historians doubt the truth of this story. Whether Osman dreamed such a dream or not, the story of his dream became the foundation that sustained the Ottoman Empire for the next six centuries. In effect, the dream said that Allah had chosen the House of Osman to conquer the world and wield authority over it—and Osman would cause the Muslim people to prosper under his reign.

Osman was a tribal chief—what the Muslims called an *emir*—who controlled a region in the northeast corner of Anatolia (the ancient name for the Turkish Peninsula). The people he ruled were called the Osmanh, the people of Osman. The word *Osmanh* later evolved to a form we recognize today: Ottoman. The Ottoman Empire is the Islamic caliphate founded by Osman I.

The Ottomans first appear in the annals of history at the Battle of Bapheus in July 1302. The battle was fought on a plain near the fortified Byzantine city of Nicomedia. Five thousand horsemen led by Osman overwhelmed a much smaller army of Byzantine foot soldiers. As a result of that first Ottoman victory, the Turkish Muslims led by Osman captured a vast region of north-central Turkey called Bithynia, and the region became an Islamic state ruled by Osman I. Over the next six centuries, that Islamic state grew, conquest by conquest, until the collapse and partitioning of the Ottoman Empire after World War I.

Historian Caroline Finkel suggests that Osman and his fellow warriors may have been driven by the Muslim doctrine of jihad. Finkel explains, "For Muslims the world was notionally divided into the 'abode of Islam,' where Islam prevailed, and the 'abode of war,' the infidel lands that must one day accept Islam—and 'holy war' was the means to bring this about. 'Holy war' had, after all, motivated the Muslim community in its early years as the new faith sought to expand and . . . had provided inspiration to fighters down the ages."[2]

Modern Turkey is a Muslim nation today in large part because of Osman's victory at the Battle of Bapheus in 1302. Before that battle, the region of Bithynia was a Byzantine stronghold populated by Christians. The Christian faith had been legalized in the Roman Empire by Constantine I in the early fourth century and was made the official state religion of the Roman Empire by Theodosius I in the late fourth century. The people of Bithynia belonged to a Christian tradition we now know as the Eastern Orthodox Church.

After the Battle of Bapheus, the Byzantine army withdrew into their forts throughout Bithynia and no longer protected the Christian population in the region. Christian churches had thrived in Bithynia since the time of the apostles, as evidenced by the apostle Peter's mentioning of Bithynia in 1 Peter 1:1. But after more than twelve centuries of Christian witness in the region, the Bithynian Christians were driven out by Muslim persecution. The Christians fled across the Bosporus (the narrow strait that divides Europe and Asia) and settled in Greece and other parts of Europe.

Once again, as in centuries past, the Christian church and the gospel of peace had been displaced by Islamic mosques and the clash of swords.

The holy wars of the sultanate

The original Islamic empire founded by Muhammad in the seventh century had begun to wane by the late tenth century. The rise of Osman I and his Ottoman army ignited a resurgence of militant, political Islam across Turkey. As the Ottoman Empire expanded beyond the borders of Asia Minor into the Middle East, Africa, and Asia, millions of people converted to Islam—some voluntarily, others by force.

In his 1938 book *The Rise of the Ottoman Empire*, Austrian historian Paul Wittek states that the expansionist Ottoman Islamic state was driven to conquer other lands and peoples by the Koran-based ideology of jihad against non-Muslims. The Ottomans referred to these holy warriors as *Ghazis*. Likewise, a nation that waged jihad against non-Muslim nations was called a Ghazi state or Ghazi emirate. Wittek quotes the Muslim poet Ahmedi, who describes the Ghazi warrior this way:

Who is a Ghazi? . . . A Ghazi is the instrument of the religion of Allah, a servant of God who purifies the earth from the filth of polytheism. . . . The Ghazi is the sword of God, he is the protector and the refuge of the believers. If he becomes a martyr in the ways of God, do not believe that he has died—he lives in beatitude with Allah, he has eternal life.[3]

Were the early Ottomans acting purely out of religious zeal and a desire to spread the Islamic faith as commanded in the Koran? Probably not. Like the Barbary pirates of the later Ottoman era, who preyed on ships and took hostages and slaves for their own profit, the early Ottomans may have merely rationalized self-serving crimes of slaughter, enslavement, and theft by viewing it as holy service to Allah. Bloodshed and torture were justified, even sanctified, if it meant that the kingdom of Islam would spread around the world.

The history of the Ottoman Empire is the history of the Second Jihad—a history of ruthless conquest and restless expansion. The armies of Osman I claimed vast tracts of territory across Anatolia (Turkey). Upon Osman's death (c. 1324), he was succeeded by Orhan, who pushed the Islamic frontier into southeastern Europe. Orhan was not only a great military strategist like Osman, but he was also an able administrator who transformed the early Ottoman sultanate into a functioning state.

Orhan died in 1360 and was succeeded by his son Murad I. A keen strategist, Murad didn't waste blood and treasure trying to capture the thick-walled fortress of Constantinople. Instead, his armies bypassed the Byzantine capital, fought northward into Europe, and conquered the Greek city of Adrianople, the second-most important city in the Byzantine Empire. Murad renamed the city Edirne and made it the capital of his sultanate. He went on to conquer Macedonia, Bulgaria, and the Balkans and divided his sultanate into two provinces—the Asian province of Anatolia and the European province of Rumelia. Murad's forces won a decisive victory over the Byzantines at the Battle of Kosovo in 1389—but Murad himself was assassinated by a traitor during the battle.

Murad's successor was his son Bayezid I, who besieged Constantinople but failed to conquer the city. In 1396, Bayezid won a decisive victory over the Crusaders at Nicopolis in Bulgaria. In 1402, his forces were defeated by the Mongol warlord Timur at the Battle of Ankara. Bayezid was captured and died a year later in captivity.

Sultan Bayezid's death and the defeat of the Ottoman army at Ankara dealt a serious blow to the Ottoman Empire. From 1402 to 1413, the Islamic empire languished, torn by a bitter power struggle and unable to expand its borders as Bayezid's sons battled each other for control of the realm. Ultimately, Bayezid's fourth son, Mehmed, was victorious.

Mehmed I consolidated his control over Anatolia and the European territories in 1413 and ruled the Ottoman Empire until his death in 1421. Under his leadership, the empire once again became aggressively warlike and expanded into new territories.

Mehmed's successor, Murad II, broke peace treaties and trade agreements with the powerful city-state of Venice, taking the Ottoman Empire to war against the Italians. Venice had established its own seaports in the Adriatic and Aegean seas, and trade with other nations in the region generated great wealth for Venetian merchants. Venice had also blocked the Ottoman advance into the Adriatic and the Aegean. By going to war against Venice, Murad II forced the Italian city-state to abandon its attempts to halt Ottoman aggression in the region.

As Mehmed conquered new territories in Europe, he enslaved

Christian youths and forced them to serve in a Muslim infantry corps called the Janissaries (or New Force). Conscripts had to convert to Islam, deny Christ, adopt all the Islamic rituals, and serve the sultan for life.

In 1444, Murad abdicated, turning the sultanate over to his twelve-year-old son, Mehmed II—though he remained a close advisor to the young sultan. Pope Eugenius IV, who was head of both the Roman church and the Holy Roman Empire, sent an army of Crusaders to push the Ottoman occupation forces out of Christian Europe. Perhaps realizing that the affairs of state and the dangers of war were too much for a boy to handle, Murad took back the reins of the sultanate from Mehmed II and led the Ottoman forces to victory over the Crusaders in the Battle of Varna on November 10, 1444. This was the Roman church's last Crusade against the Ottoman Empire.

Murad went on to establish and consolidate Ottoman rule over Macedonia, Bulgaria, Greece, and Thrace (a region made up of parts of modern Bulgaria, Greece, and European Turkey). By the time Murad died in 1451, the Danube River in Europe formed the northern border of the Ottoman Empire.

Blood and terror in the streets

After Murad's death, Mehmed II returned to the throne, and he was eager to conquer more territory in the name of Islam. His first goal was the conquest of the fortified city of Constantinople, the longtime capital of the Byzantine Empire, which had long resisted Ottoman sieges and attacks. Mehmed constructed the Rumeli Fortress on the European shore of the Bosporus. It served as a forward staging area for the siege of Constantinople, which began on April 6, 1453, when Mehmed was twenty-one years old.

The siege of Constantinople opened with an Ottoman cannon barrage of the city's thick walls; but the cannon fire had little effect. The Ottoman fleet was eager to enter an estuary and harbor called the Golden Horn that ran through the center of the city, but the army of Constantinople under Emperor Constantine XI Palaiologos blocked the entrance to the Golden Horn with a massive chain.

Mehmed responded by constructing an overland road made of greased logs, stretching from the Bosporus Strait to a stream that fed into the Golden Horn. On April 22, the sailors of Mehmed's navy dragged their ships onto this greased road, pulled them overland north of the city, and pushed them into the waters of the Golden Horn, bypassing the chain barrier. In this way, the Ottomans were able to control the waters surrounding the city, cutting the city off from being resupplied.

On the night of April 28, sailors from Constantinople set out in fire ships—vessels that were deliberately set ablaze and steered into enemy ships as weapons. The Ottomans spotted the approaching fire ships and shot at them before their crews could set them ablaze. The Byzantine crews were forced to abandon their sinking ships and were captured by the Ottomans when they reached the shore.

Mehmed ordered the captive sailors executed by impaling them on vertical stakes in full view of the city walls. Victims sometimes took days to die from this cruel and painful torture.

In retaliation, Constantine XI ordered the execution of 260 Ottoman prisoners on the city walls.

Next, Mehmed sent his army in wave after wave of frontal assaults against the walls of Constantinople, and his army suffered incredible losses. The Ottomans refused to leave their dead on the battlefield and would brave the gunfire and crossbow arrows of the city defenders to retrieve the bodies of the fallen. Many soldiers who went out to retrieve the dead ended up dead as well. Mehmed seemed to have an inexhaustible supply of soldiers to hurl against the walls of Constantinople.

In mid-May, the Ottomans dug tunnels to smuggle explosives under the walls to blow them up. The city defenders discovered the Ottoman plan and put a stop to the enemy tunnels.

On May 21, Mehmed sent a message to Constantine XI, offering to spare the lives of the people if they would surrender the city. He also offered to allow the emperor to retain a measure of power as a local governor under Ottoman authority. Emperor Constantine replied that the people of the city preferred death over dishonor.

The Ottomans immediately began preparations for a massive assault on the city. Mehmed II promised his soldiers that, after the city had been conquered, he would give them freedom to plunder the city and deal with the populace as they wished for three days and nights.[4]

Emperor Constantine, meanwhile, began preparing his people for the approaching onslaught. On May 28, he called for a prayer vigil and a worship service at the beautiful domed Hagia Sophia (the Church of Holy Wisdom), which at the time was the largest Christian house of worship in the world. Both Roman and Eastern Orthodox clerics participated in the service.

A little after midnight, the Ottomans launched an all-out

assault against the city gates and walls. Wave after wave of troops threw themselves at the city, concentrating on a stretch of cannon-damaged wall on the northwest side of the city. After hours of fighting and absorbing heavy losses, the Ottoman forces broke through the wall, only to be turned back by a strong force of defenders inside the city.

Finally, Mehmed sent a corps of highly trained infantry, called Janissaries, through the breach in the wall. The officer in charge of Constantinople's troops, General Giovanni Giustiniani, from the Italian city of Genoa, was wounded in the assault. When the troops saw their general being carried out of the battle, they panicked and fell back, allowing the Ottomans to flood into the city.

At that point, Emperor Constantine knew that his cause was lost—yet he stood at the front line, sword in hand, and rallied his troops to stand and fight as the Ottoman Janissaries battled their way into the city. Leading the defense of the city, Constantine XI died in the streets of Constantinople with his men.

Before the city was completely overrun, Constantinople's allies from Venice and Genoa broke the chain that blocked the Golden Horn, boarded their ships, and sailed away. Within the city walls, the Ottomans killed many Christians and took others captive as slaves. The Ottoman soldiers, with the blessing of Mehmed, looted the homes and shops of the city.

As the Ottoman forces filled the Augusteum, the stone-paved plaza in front of the Hagia Sophia, several thousand citizens of Constantinople huddled together in prayer behind the massive bronze doors of the church. Undeterred, the Ottomans broke down the doors and hauled out the Christians to be sold into slavery. The invaders then plundered the sanctuary, taking anything of value, desecrating altars and images, and parading through the streets holding up stolen crucifixes in mockery of the Christian faith.

In the streets of Constantinople, the Ottoman troops randomly slaughtered men, women, and children and took others as slaves. The plundering of the city continued for three days and nights. Some Ottoman soldiers fought each other to the death over possession of the spoils.

Niccolò Barbaro, a Venetian doctor, was a survivor and eyewitness of the fall of Constantinople. He later wrote, "The blood flowed in the city like rainwater in the gutters after a sudden storm, and the corpses of Turks and Christians were thrown into the Dardanelles, where they floated out to sea like melons on a canal."[5]

On June 21, three weeks after the fall of Constantinople, Sultan Mehmed II rode on horseback through the city, accompanied by his advisors. The city was largely in ruins, burned and deserted, lifeless and silent. Churches were desolate, houses uninhabited, stores and shops stripped to the walls. Surveying the devastation his army had committed, the Sultan wept and said, "What a city we have given over to plunder and destruction!"[6]

Though the Hagia Sophia had been looted and desecrated, it still stood. Constructed between 532 and 537 by order of the Byzantine emperor Justinian I, the church had been dedicated to the Wisdom of God, the *Logos*, the second person of the Trinity. By order of Mehmed II, it was declared an Islamic mosque on May 29, 1453, the day of the fall of

Constantinople. It remained a mosque until 1931, when it was turned into a museum.

The fall of Constantinople dealt a devastating blow to the Christian West. In a single day, the Byzantine Empire came to an end—and so did the Crusades. Though several European monarchs and Roman Catholic popes talked about launching a Crusade to reconquer Constantinople, no Crusaders ever again went forth to reclaim territory lost in the Second Jihad.

Constantinople remained in Muslim hands and became the capital of the Ottoman Empire until the empire itself collapsed following World War I. Today, Constantinople is called Istanbul, and it is still Turkey's largest city.

If there is any silver lining to the fall of Constantinople, perhaps it is this: The demise of the Byzantine Empire and its capital triggered a mass migration of Greek scholars, scientists, philosophers, artists, and writers out of the regions that were controlled or threatened by the Ottomans. Most moved to the Italian city-states, such as Milan, Venice, Florence, Genoa, and Pisa. There they enriched the culture of fifteenth-century Italy, encouraged the revival of classical Greek learning, and helped bring Europe out of the Dark Ages into the Renaissance. When Martin Luther published his Ninety-Five Theses in 1517, igniting the Protestant Reformation, the enlightened thought of both the Renaissance and the Reformation combined to produce what we now call Western civilization.

The bloody reign of Mehmed the Conqueror

Mehmed II went on to rule the Ottoman Empire for more than thirty years, and his reign was characterized by a state of almost constant warfare—wars of jihad, wars of Islamic conquest. The mapmakers of the time couldn't keep up with Mehmed's conquests—Serbia, Morea, the coast of the Black Sea, Wallachia, Bosnia, Karaman, Albania, Crimea. As a result of these victories, he became known as Mehmed the Conqueror.

Mehmed had five wives and four children, and he was notorious for his sexual abuse of children and for murdering those who refused his sexual advances. One incident involved Loukas Notaras, the last *megas doux* (grand duke or prime minister) of the Byzantine Empire under Constantine XI. After the fall of Constantinople, Mehmed treated Notaras and his family with respect—when Mehmed was sober. Scottish historian Patrick Balfour (Lord Kinross) describes in his book *The Ottoman Centuries* what Mehmed did when he was drunk:

> One evening at a banquet Mehmed, who was well flushed
> with wine, as was often his habit, and who was known to have
> ambivalent sexual tastes, sent a eunuch to the house of Notaras,
> demanding that he supply his good-looking fourteen-year-old
> son for the Sultan's pleasure. When [Notaras] refused, the Sultan
> instantly ordered the decapitation of Notaras, together with that
> of his son and his son-in-law; and their three heads, so it is related,
> were placed on the banqueting table before him.[7]

A slightly different description of the execution of Notaras and his sons was recorded by Nikolaos Sekoundinos, a Greek from Venice who visited Constantinople in the summer of 1453, just weeks after the city fell, and interviewed survivors of the battle. In writing an account of the fall of the city, Sekoundinos makes a point of the deep Christian commitment of Loukas Notaras and his family:

> [Sultan Mehmed] summoned and sent for [Notaras's] young son. . . . [Notaras] realized that his young son was being summoned to participate in the unspeakable vice. And so he refused to obey the summons and said that he would rather die than subject his little boy to such perversion. . . . [Mehmed] became angry and ordered that the son be snatched away from the arms and embraces of his parents and be hauled before him. He condemned Loukas, his two other sons, and his son-in-law to death. . . . [Notaras] decided that a brave and notable man must accept glorious death. He feared though, that once he, the father, had died, his sons and son-in-law, because of their age and tender minds, would choose to live by committing a most foul crime and deny their most sacred faith through conversion [to Islam]. So he asked the executioner to slaughter his sons and son-in-law first and then execute him. . . .
>
> [Notaras] strengthened the spirits of his sons and of his son-in-law, and affected them in such a way that they stretched their necks for the ax with a joyful mind and with eager disposition they piously committed their souls to the Creator. . . . [Then Notaras] invited the executioner to perform his duty. [The executioner] miserably executed that wonderful man of steadfast faith.[8]

The moral courage and spiritual strength of this Christian family inspires and challenges us. If you and I are ever called to endure persecution in the Third Jihad, will we stand as confidently and resolutely as Loukas Notaras and his family? The time for building our Christian character and strengthening our faith is *now*. Only if Christ is the absolute Lord of our lives *today* will we stand firm for him in the time of testing.

In 1481, Mehmed set off on a new campaign with his Ottoman army to invade the Greek island of Rhodes, off the Turkish coast. From there he planned to invade southern Italy. Some historians believe he intended to overthrow the sultanate of Egypt and establish a caliphate stretching from Europe to Asia to Africa. However, during the journey, Mehmed fell ill and died at the age of forty-nine. When news of his death reached Christian Europe, church bells pealed the news and people celebrated in the streets.

Expand and conquer

Political Islam's three primary targets were Jerusalem (the city of David and the Messiah), Rome (the city of the Western church), and Constantinople (the city of the Eastern church). The Islamic caliphate of Umar ibn al-Khattab conquered Jerusalem in 638 during the First Jihad. The Ottoman Turks under Mehmed the Conqueror took Constantinople in 1453 during the Second Jihad. Rome, however, has remained out of reach. Though Ottoman rulers made many attempts to invade Italy, they were stopped each time. Mehmed the Conqueror's plan to invade Italy was thwarted by his unexpected death. Later Ottoman sultans attempted to invade the Italian Peninsula but were unable to overcome the fierce Albanian resistance that blocked their path. Nevertheless, political Islam remains obsessed to this day with conquering Rome and raising the Islamic flag over the dome of the Vatican.

We saw a bloody, senseless demonstration of this obsession in early 2015 when twenty-one Egyptian Coptic Christian construction workers, kidnapped from the city of Sirte in Libya, were lined up on a Libyan beach and beheaded. The terror organization ISIS released a five-minute video of the mass beheadings on February 15. The video was titled "A message signed with blood to the nations of the Cross." The executed men were identified as "People of the Cross, followers of the hostile Egyptian Church," and the killers called themselves the Tripoli Province of ISIS.

After the murders, the masked speaker in the video pointed his bloody knife toward the Mediterranean Sea, toward Rome, and said, "We will conquer Rome, by Allah's permission." The message of the video is unmistakable: The Islamists spilled Christian blood into the sea so that it would flow toward Rome, a declaration of war against all of Christendom.

Following the death of Mehmed the Conqueror, the Ottoman Empire continued to expand its boundaries through holy wars. Sultan Selim I (1512-1520) pushed out the eastern and southern borders and achieved Mehmed's unfulfilled dream of establishing Ottoman control of Egypt. Suleiman the Magnificent (1520–1566) conquered the kingdom we now know as Hungary and twice tried to conquer Vienna in Austria. Suleiman also sent his forces eastward to drive the Persians out of Baghdad in 1535, giving the Ottomans a port on the Persian Gulf as well as control of Mesopotamia. By 1560, the Ottoman Empire ruled Somalia and the Horn of Africa and was competing with Portugal for mastery of the Indian Ocean.

Historians Gábor Ágoston and Bruce Masters offer an

assessment of Suleiman's expansion of the Ottoman Empire: "His conquests substantially expanded the empire's territories from 576,900 square miles in 1520 to 877,888 square miles in 1566, an increase of more than 50 percent. His most important conquests, central Hungary and Iraq, were seized from his two formidable opponents, the Habsburgs and Safavids."[9]

By 1600, the Ottoman Empire controlled much of North Africa—the region that would spawn the dreaded Barbary pirates. From the Atlantic Ocean to the Indian Ocean, the Ottomans were a political and military power to be reckoned with for all European nations.

The gates of Vienna

In 1683, Grand Vizier Kara Mustafa Pasha and Sultan Mehmed IV led an army of one hundred thousand soldiers in a new Ottoman attack against Austria. Forces included soldiers from every corner of the Ottoman Empire. When the Austrian emperor, Leopold I, heard of the advancing Islamic army, he knew that Vienna was their objective. A week before the Ottomans arrived, Leopold and his court packed up the wealth and treasures of Vienna and fled 137 miles west to the city of Passau. On July 14, when the Ottomans reached Vienna, they sent a messenger to the city gates, calling on the Christians to accept Islam, turn over the fortress in peace, or face death or enslavement.

The commander of the twelve thousand soldiers of Vienna refused to parlay with the Islamic army. Word had come of a similar offer the Ottomans had made to the village of Perchtoldsdorf only a few days earlier. When the Christians in that village had surrendered, the Ottomans had slaughtered them all.

By July 17, the Ottomans surrounded Vienna and began their siege. The people of Vienna were trapped behind their walls throughout July and the month of August. As the supply of drinking water ran low, filth piled up in the streets, and cholera and typhus afflicted the terrified people. The Ottomans moved their siege lines closer and closer to the walls, raining cannon fire upon the city. By early September, the twelve thousand soldiers guarding the walls had been reduced to three thousand, and breaches in the walls were beginning to appear.

What neither the people of Vienna nor the Ottoman forces knew was that a relief army of sixty thousand Christian soldiers was approaching the city. Commanded by King John III Sobieski of Poland, the reinforcements were moving toward the besieged city through the Vienna Woods—a dense highland forest. The Ottomans had left that side of the city undefended, believing that no army could pass through the tangled, mountainous woods.

On Sunday morning, September 12, the Polish army emerged from the woods, and King John led his army in a charge against the unprepared Ottoman encampment. The forces of Kara Mustafa and Sultan Mehmed IV scrambled to get to their weapons and form a counterattack, and within hours the Ottomans were fleeing the battlefield in panic and disarray.

King John III Sobieski later wrote—paraphrasing the famous words of Julius Caesar—"We came, we saw, and God conquered." The defeat at the gates of Vienna dealt a devastating blow to the Ottoman Empire—the first step toward decades of steady decline by the Islamic realm. With profound suddenness, the Ottomans' seemingly unstoppable expansion was brought to a halt.

The legacy of the Ottoman Empire is not entirely one of barbarism, bloodshed, and conquest. There were times when the empire demonstrated compassion toward the Christian and Jewish communities. In 1840, for example, Ottoman Sultan Abdülmecid donated one thousand pounds of sterling to Ireland to alleviate hunger during the potato famine. But the Ottoman Empire was also responsible for the Armenian genocide of 1915 to 1923, when the Turks systematically exterminated 1.5 million Christian Armenians. This mass murder was accompanied by death marches, forced labor, mass deportations, starvation, robbery, and rape. The Ottomans frequently employed cruelty as a matter of state policy—and as a weapon of jihad.

Down but not out

In 1899, as the era of the Ottoman Empire and Second Jihad drew to a close, Winston Churchill wrote about the state of the Muslim religion at that time—and his words hold an ominous currency for the times we live in today:

> The fact that in Mohammedan law every woman must *belong* to some man as his absolute property—either as a child, a wife, or a concubine—must delay the final extinction of slavery until the faith of Islam has ceased to be a great power among men. Individual Moslems may show splendid qualities . . . but the influence of the religion paralyses the social development

of those who follow it. No stronger retrograde force exists in the world. Far from being moribund, Mohammedanism is a militant and proselytising faith. It has already spread throughout Central Africa, raising fearless warriors at every step; and were it not that Christianity is sheltered in the strong arms of science—the science against which it had vainly struggled—the civilisation of modern Europe might fall, as fell the civilisation of ancient Rome.[10]

In other words, Islam's treatment of women is tantamount to slavery, and the tenets of Islam stifle social and cultural advancement, keeping its followers stuck in the past. Yet Islam continually seeks to spread, and the only thing that keeps Islam from taking over Europe is the rational, enlightened faith that is Christianity—a faith that (unlike Islam) harmonizes with science and reason.

But Churchill's words are ominous precisely because Christianity—which he believed was a bulwark against the advance of Islam into Europe—is largely dead across Europe and Great Britain. The Christian church in Europe is essentially irrelevant, a formal institution that no longer preaches or practices the gospel of Jesus Christ. If Churchill was counting on Christianity as Europe's best hope for withstanding the coming Islamic jihad, what hope is there now that so many European churches are empty and dark?

The Ottoman Empire collapsed after World War I, when its territories were partitioned by the Treaty of Sèvres. The Ottoman Sultanate was abolished in 1922, and the caliphate was abolished in 1924. This was the end of the Second Jihad, but it was not the end of the ancient goal of a worldwide Islamic State. A decade and a half later, Catholic historian Hilaire Belloc, a longtime friend and associate of G. K. Chesterton's, wrote a book called *The Great Heresies*, in which he predicted that Islam would rise again in our time:

> It has always seemed to me possible, and even probable, that there would be a resurrection of Islam and that our sons or our grandsons would see the renewal of that tremendous struggle between the Christian culture and what has been for more than a thousand years its greatest opponent. . . .
>
> It is indeed a vital question, "May not Islam arise again?"
>
> In a sense the question is already answered because Islam has never departed. It still commands the fixed loyalty and unquestioning adhesion of all the millions between the Atlantic and the Indus and further afield throughout scattered communities of further Asia. But I ask the question in the sense, "Will not perhaps the temporal power of Islam return and with it the menace of an armed Mohammedan world which will shake off the domination of Europeans—still nominally Christian— and reappear again as the prime enemy of our civilization?" The future always comes as a surprise, but political wisdom consists in attempting at least some partial judgment of what that surprise may be. And for my part I cannot but believe that a main unexpected thing of the future is the return of Islam. . . . We are in the presence of an unstable equilibrium which cannot remain permanently unstable. . . .
>
> In view of this, anyone with a knowledge of history is bound to ask himself whether we shall not see in the future a revival of

Mohammedan political power, and the renewal of the old pressure of Islam upon Christendom.[11]

During the First and Second Jihads, Islamic empires fought wars of conquest against the Christian West. But is it still accurate to say that Western civilization is *Christian*? News and entertainment media in the West openly mock the Christian virtues of truth, faith, and morality. Western universities teach our young people to despise the Bible and Christian values. Western governments have begun silencing and punishing Christians who are vocal about their faith or who take a moral stand for the biblical view of marriage and morality. Many churches have departed from the good news of Jesus Christ and now preach a false gospel of accommodation to the surrounding godless culture.

The next time the armies of Islam reach the gates of Vienna or any other Western city, who will stand ready to oppose them? Where are the courageous, committed Christians who will stand for God's truth against the forces of jihad? I'm not suggesting that Christians should arm themselves for a violent new Crusade—God forbid! I am saying that we in the community of faith need to encourage each other and challenge each other to stand firmly, boldly, and publicly for truth.

The goal of Islamic conquest has remained unchanged year after year, century after century, right up to our own era. In 1979, after the Islamic revolutionaries seized power in Iran, their spiritual leader, Ayatollah Khomeini, declared, "The governments of the world should know that Islam cannot be defeated. Islam will be victorious in all countries of the world, and Islam and the teachings of the Koran will prevail all over the world."[12] Khomeini merely reiterated what Islamist leaders have voiced for centuries and still voice today.

While the United States battled Islamic insurgents in Iraq in 2005, Jordanian militant Abu Musab al-Zarqawi, then head of al-Qaeda in Iraq, released a statement explaining the aims of his terrorist organization: "We are not fighting to chase out the occupier or to save national unity and keep the borders outlined by the infidels intact. We are fighting because it is a religious duty to do it, just as it is a duty to take the Sharia [Islamic law] to the government and create an Islamic state."[13]

Fourteen centuries have passed since Muhammad stepped out of the darkness of a desert cave to announce his vision of a world surrendered and submitted to the demands of his new religion. The goals of Islamic fundamentalism have not changed one degree in all that time.

7

THE THIRD JIHAD HAS BEGUN

ON SUNDAY MORNING, MAY 13, 2018, a Muslim family in Surabaya, Indonesia, went on a murderous jihad against their Christian neighbors. A father, a mother, and their four children divided up into teams and suicide-bombed three separate churches for no other reason than to kill Christians. The attacks took place in Indonesia's second-largest city, killing a dozen Christians and all six members of the Muslim family. More than forty people were injured.

The terrorist family used three methods of attack. The father drove an explosives-laden van to the Pentecost Central Church and detonated the bomb out front. The mother walked into the Indonesian Christian Church with her two daughters, ages nine and twelve, and set off a hidden suicide vest. (I wonder: Did those two girls know that their mother was about to murder them?) The couple's two teenage sons rode a pair of motorcycles up to Santa Maria Catholic Church and simultaneously triggered their suicide vests.

A Muslim neighbor of the family later told reporters, "We were not suspicious of anything because they are a family that is well known and normal."[1]

The Islamic State (ISIS) boasted that it was responsible for the attacks, which it described as acts of martyrdom. The Indonesian government identified the parents as belonging to Jamaah Ansharut Daulah, a terror group affiliated with ISIS, which has been aggressively recruiting in Indonesia in recent years. Indonesia is the most populous Muslim country in the world, with 261 million people. The population is roughly four-fifths Muslim and one-tenth Christian.[2]

Many Americans are under the mistaken impression that terrorism and jihadism are fueled by poverty and oppression in the Muslim world, but the facts don't support this notion. Most terrorists come from economically advantaged families and are well-educated. According to the Associated Press, the Muslim family that carried out the three horrifying suicide attacks against Christians in Surabaya was no exception. The father had a good income, and the family lived in an upper-middle-class residential community called Wonorejo Asri.[3]

Researchers Efraim Benmelech, from the Kellogg School of Management at Northwestern University, and Esteban Klor, from the Department of Economics at the Hebrew University of Jerusalem, conducted extensive research into the reasons people join ISIS and similar Islamist death cults. Their conclusion:

Poor economic conditions do not drive participation in ISIS. In contrast, the number of ISIS foreign fighters is positively correlated with a country's GDP per capita and Human Development Index (HDI). Many foreign fighters originate from countries with high levels of economic development, low income inequality, and highly developed political institutions. . . . Our results suggest that the flow of foreign fighters to ISIS is not driven by economic or political conditions but rather by ideology and the difficulty of assimilation into homogeneous Western countries.[4]

The Indonesian terrorist family clearly fits this pattern.

A father, a mother, teenagers, and even preteen children—are these the foot soldiers of the Third Jihad? What sort of religion turns a family of six into a team of jihadist mass murderers? How did this Islamist cult of death get started?

The origins of the Third Jihad

The story of the First Jihad began with Muhammad, the founder of Islam. The story of the Second Jihad began with Osman I, the founder of the Ottoman Empire. To understand the Third Jihad, we must begin with an Egyptian man named Sayyid Qutb. Most Westerners have never heard of him, yet our civilization has been strongly (and negatively) affected by his ideas and his writings. It's fair to say that the terror attacks of 9/11 might never have happened if Sayyid Qutb had never been born. His life exemplifies the cultural clash between political Islam and Western civilization.

Born in 1906, Qutb was a Sunni Muslim scholar, literary critic, and political activist. In 1949, he came to the United

States to study literature and culture at Colorado State Teachers College in Greeley. His two-year stay in Greeley had a profound influence on his view of Western culture in general and especially American culture. Greeley was a typical example of small-town America, populated by mostly upright, conservative, churchgoing people. It was, in fact, a dry town that prohibited liquor sales long after the repeal of Prohibition.

To Sayyid Qutb, however, Greeley was a shocking Sodom-like cesspool of vice and depravity. Some of his disgust with American society is understandable. For example, he was offended by the racism and segregation that were a fact of life in parts of America. As an Arab Muslim, he was also angered by America's support for the newly founded state of Israel. But he was also horrified by aspects of American life that we take for granted—such as lush green lawns. It offended him, as a son of the desert, to see lawn sprinklers showering gallons of water onto residential lawns, which then had to be mowed and edged every Saturday. Such extravagant waste!

Qutb also expressed a distorted perspective on American history. In a 1951 article titled "Amrika Allati Ra'itu" ("The America I Have Seen"), he described what he viewed as America's hunger for war:

> The American is by his very nature a warrior who loves combat. The idea of combat and war runs strong in his blood. It is evident in his manner and this is what agrees with his history. For the first waves of people left their homelands, heading for America with the intention of building and competing and struggling. And once there, some of them killed others, as they were composed

of groups and factions. Then they all fought against the original inhabitants of the land (the red Indians), and they continue to wage a bloody war against them until this very moment. Then the Anglo-Saxons killed the Latinos and pushed them south toward central and southern America. Then these Americanized people turned against their mother country, England, in a destructive war led by George Washington until they obtained their independence from the British crown. . . .

Then the North fought the South under the command of Abraham Lincoln in a war that was called "the freeing of the slaves." But its true motivation was economic competition. The slaves that had been captured from central Africa to work in the land were fragile and could not withstand the cold climate of the North, so they were moved to the South. The result was that the builders of the South found cheap labor that was unavailable in the North. So they achieved economic superiority. For this reason, the Northerners declared war for the manumission of the slaves![5]

Qutb expressed his view that Western notions of freedom, human rights, and democracy are not compatible with Islam. He divided the world into two warring cultures, Islam and *jahiliyya* (pre-Islamic ignorance). He called for all Muslims to return to a pure, seventh-century form of Islam, saying, "We need to initiate the movement of Islamic revival."[6] His writings became popular throughout the Islamic community, and his views spread rapidly around the world. Today, he is revered as "the father of modern [Islamic] fundamentalism."[7] Terrorist leaders Osama bin Laden and Ayman al-Zawahiri cite Sayyid Qutb as a role model and a hero.

After returning home to Egypt, Qutb joined the Muslim Brotherhood. In 1954, the Egyptian government arrested him for conspiring to assassinate Egyptian president Gamal Abdel Nasser. While in prison, Qutb wrote his manifesto, *Ma'alim fi al-Tariq* (*Milestones*), which he smuggled out of the prison with the help of friends. The book received wide circulation despite the government's attempt to suppress it.

Eventually, Qutb was released from prison, but he was soon arrested again and charged with plotting to overthrow the Egyptian government. When he was convicted and sentenced to death, he told the court, "I performed jihad for fifteen years until I earned this martyrdom."[8] He was hanged in 1966, and his writings continue to inspire jihadists today.

A minority of one

Hussein Aboubakr was born in 1989 and raised in a middle-class Muslim family in Cairo, Egypt. His parents and teachers taught him that the Islamic religion and culture are superior to all others, that Christians are "crusaders" and enemies, and that Jews are the embodiment of all that is evil in the world. As a boy, he was taught to fear and hate the Jews because they drink the blood of Muslim children.

These messages were reinforced in young Hussein's home, at school, at the mosque, and in Egyptian movies and TV shows. There was even an Egyptian comic book character called Man of the Impossible, who battled Jewish supervillains and Zionist conspiracies. Inspired by these myths, Hussein Aboubakr dreamed of becoming an Islamic warrior in the battle against Israel. He began studying the Hebrew language over the Internet, intending one day to infiltrate the Israeli conspiracies.

"Growing up," he said, "I was told, among many other things, that every day that passes in the Islamic nation without a caliphate is a sin. That the failures and miseries of the Muslim world started the moment we Muslims gave up conquests and wars against the infidels. That our prosperity depended on conquering new lands and converting new believers. That anyone who leaves the faith must die. And I also remember how my teachers and my mosque imams reacted to the news of 9/11 when it happened: *joy*."[9]

As Hussein studied the Hebrew language, he began to discover Jewish history, and he was shocked by what he learned. Neither his parents nor his teachers had ever told him that the Jewish people had ancient ties to the land known as Israel and the city of Jerusalem. He had always been taught that Palestine and Jerusalem were Muslim lands, and that the Jews were invaders and occupiers. As he read about the history of anti-Semitism—the unreasoning hatred of the Jews, the pogroms of past centuries, the Holocaust of the twentieth century—it dawned on him that he had grown up surrounded by it.

He found himself rethinking everything his parents, teachers, and culture had taught him. What if women *weren't* inferior to men? What if it was morally wrong to persecute and oppress the 10 million Coptic Christians in Egypt? What if it was morally wrong to hate and exterminate the Jews? He now feared that everyone around him believed a pack of lies and nonsense. Yet he also feared that he was crazy, that he was the only person in Egypt who had such doubts. Was the insanity within him, in his doubting mind—or was the insanity all around him, in Islamic culture?

He read Western literature, trying to gain an outside perspective on his own culture and the world. He identified with Winston Smith, the hero of George Orwell's novel *1984*. Smith lived in a totalitarian society awash with propaganda and lies. Hussein was struck by a notion Winston Smith expressed in the novel: "Perhaps a lunatic was simply a minority of one."[10] Hussein realized he wasn't crazy. He was simply a minority of one. It was his culture that was crazy.

At his university, Hussein Aboubakr studied the Hebrew language and literature, but his Muslim instructors taught Jewish history from a Muslim perspective. Eager to know the truth, he supplemented his studies with trips to the Israeli Academic Center in Cairo (affiliated with the Israeli embassy), where he read Israeli literature and newspapers. He soon discovered, however, that the Egyptian government had him under surveillance and was tapping his phone.

Finally, the police arrested Hussein and his father, accusing them both of treason and reminding them about the "evil ways" of the Jews. Both men were finally released, but Hussein's father was furious with him for getting them into trouble with the police. Hussein admitted to his family that he no longer believed in the Islamic view of Jews, Christians, and the inferiority of women. His father and brother threw him out of the house.

In January 2011, Hussein Aboubakr took part in the Tahrir Square protests that led to the downfall of Egyptian president Hosni Mubarak. The police arrested Hussein and placed him in a prison camp for several weeks. Upon his release, he sought political asylum in the United States. Today, he lives in California and is an outspoken advocate for Israel—a nation, he says, that "gives hope that the Middle East can have Western, moral values with human rights, liberty, and freedom."[11]

Hussein Aboubakr is living proof that truth can penetrate the wall of lies that surrounds and imprisons the Muslim mind.

Three types of Muslims

There are many different denominations of Islam—the two dominant sects, Sunni and Shia, plus lesser-known sects such as Sufism, Ahmadiyya, Ibadi, and Mahdavia. For our purposes here, let's consider three essential types of Muslims: *moderate Muslims*, *militant Muslims*, and *political Muslims*.

1. *Moderate Muslims* comprise a portion of the Muslim population—but how many moderate Muslims are there? It depends on how you define *moderate*, and the results may vary by country of origin. For example, a 2013 study by the Pew Research Center found that 74 percent of Egyptian Muslims believe that everyone in the country, both Muslims and non-Muslims, should be subject to Sharia law—hardly a moderate attitude. In Iraq, by contrast, only 38 percent of Muslims hold this view, and in Morocco, only 29 percent. In countries such as Pakistan, Afghanistan, Egypt, Malaysia, and the Palestinian territories, large majorities of those who want their country to be ruled by Islamic law also support the use of *hudud* punishments (such as public lashings and the amputation of the hands of thieves).[12]

I have known many people I consider to be moderate Muslims,

and some have explained their thinking to me. Moderate Muslims believe that the harsher, more militant passages of the Koran were for an earlier era and should not be interpreted literally today. Moderate Muslims believe in peaceful coexistence with Christians, Jews, and Western culture as a whole. They tend to accept American constitutional principles of freedom of religion, free speech, and a free press and have no desire to impose Sharia law on non-Muslims.

My guess—and it's only a guess—is that of the 1.8 billion Muslims in the world, moderates are probably in the minority. Even if that is so, there are certainly millions of moderate Muslims in the world—in our cities, our neighborhoods, working alongside us, or teaching or attending classes on our campus. They are not our enemy. They are our mission field.

2. *Militant Muslims* seek the full implementation of Sharia law and a global Islamic caliphate. They are willing to use any and all means, including violence and terrorism, to achieve their goals. Militant Muslims include members and supporters of Hezbollah and Hamas (organizations that regularly launch rocket attacks and terror attacks against Israel) and Islamist organizations such as Boko Haram, al-Shabaab, al-Qaeda, and ISIS, which use military-style attacks, hijackings, suicide attacks (martyrdom operations), bombings, kidnappings, and highly publicized executions to achieve their goals.

In 2014, the *New York Times* published an investigative report by Rukmini Callimachi, showing that between 2008 and 2013, al-Qaeda and its affiliated terror groups reaped more than $125 million from ransoms paid by Western countries for the return of European kidnap victims, mostly from Spain, France, and Switzerland. This is the same cruel fund-raising scheme the Barbary pirates used against American and European citizens in the seventeenth and eighteenth centuries.[13]

What percentage of the Muslim world is militant? It's hard to say. There are Muslims who would never join a terrorist group or commit an act of violence in the name of Islam but who still would be happy to hear of another 9/11-style attack against America or Israel. I would guess that truly militant Muslims are probably a minority within the Muslim community.

3. *Political Muslims*, like militant Muslims, believe Islam is engaged in a struggle for world domination. As I define these terms, political Muslims and militant Muslims have essentially the same goals—a global caliphate ruled by the Koran and Sharia law—but they differ in the means and methods they use to achieve those goals. While the militants are willing to use force and terror to conquer Western society, political Muslims prefer to use the Western political and legal systems to achieve those goals. Political Muslims often sound like moderate Muslims, or deceptively pose as moderate Muslims. They believe in coexistence with the West as a temporary strategy to pursue while Islam steadily increases its power and expands its territory, always with an ultimate goal of conquest.

Political Muslims believe in exercising the freedoms guaranteed by the US Constitution as a means of replacing the Constitution with Sharia law. They believe in using the democratic process to put Islamists in positions of influence and power, with a goal of eventually replacing our American democracy with an Islamic state. This is the primary strategy of the Third Jihad. The First and Second Jihads were fought with swords and siege towers. The Third Jihad is being fought with public relations and Internet technology. It's a holy war of words, of stealth, of lies.

In June 1991, Siraj Wahhaj became the first Muslim to deliver an opening prayer before the United States House of Representatives. The following year, Wahhaj spoke at a Muslim gathering in New Jersey, stating bluntly that Muslims will ultimately substitute the Koran and the caliphate in place of the Constitution. "If we were united and strong," he added, "we'd elect our own emir [president of the United States] and give allegiance to him. . . . If six to eight million Muslims unite in America, the country will come to us."[14]

The Council on American–Islamic Relations (CAIR) is, in my view, a political Muslim organization. CAIR advocates for the Muslim viewpoint in American media and the government. I believe CAIR uses First Amendment freedoms and American political institutions in a bid to eventually conquer Western society for Islam. This is not just my view but also the view of a number of *genuinely moderate* Muslims, as historian Daniel Pipes observes:

> The late Seifeldin Ashmawy, publisher of the New Jersey-based *Voice of Peace*, called CAIR the champion of "extremists whose views do not represent Islam." Jamal Hasan of the Council for Democracy and Tolerance explains that CAIR's goal is to spread "Islamic hegemony the world over by hook or by crook." Kamal Nawash, head of Free Muslims Against Terrorism, finds that

CAIR and similar groups condemn terrorism on the surface while endorsing an ideology that helps foster extremism, adding that "almost all of their members are theocratic Muslims who reject secularism and want to establish Islamic states." . . . And Stephen Schwartz of the Center on Islamic Pluralism writes that "CAIR should be considered a foreign-based subversive organization, comparable in the Islamist field to the Soviet-controlled Communist Party, USA."[15]

After the 9/11 attacks, the Federal Bureau of Investigation consulted with CAIR, which the Bureau considered a moderate group promoting Muslim-American understanding. In April 2009, however, the FBI notified the Senate Judiciary Subcommittee on Terrorism and Homeland Security that it had broken ties with CAIR. Why? Evidence showed that CAIR and its founders were clandestinely promoting the Muslim Brotherhood and Hamas. CAIR has also been listed by one Muslim nation, the United Arab Emirates, as a terrorist organization.[16]

One of the more troubling examples of CAIR's effort to wage cultural jihad in America came to light in 2017—and it involved targeting the minds and hearts of American schoolchildren. In April of that year, CAIR contacted the San Diego Unified School District with a complaint that Muslim students had been bullied in San Diego schools. District officials invited CAIR to advise them in creating programs and policies to prevent future bullying of Muslim students.

CAIR helped the school district devise a plan that involved purchasing books and other materials on Muslim beliefs for school libraries, creating Islamic clubs and Muslim "safe spaces" on high school campuses, expanding staff calendars to include Muslim holidays, and teaching school staff about Muslim culture.

The San Diego school system already had a broad-based anti-bullying program in place. But CAIR convinced school officials that they needed a *special* anti-bullying program focused *solely* on the Muslim religion and culture. CAIR's plan to attack the bullying problem involved teaching all San Diego school children CAIR's version of the history and tenets of Islam.

In response, the Freedom of Conscience Defense Fund filed suit against the school district on behalf of San Diego parents. The suit claimed that the district's Islam-centered instruction violated the First Amendment's prohibition of the establishment of a state-endorsed religion. In response to the lawsuit, the school district publicly voted to sever ties with CAIR—but attorneys for the Defense Fund uncovered hundreds of pages of emails proving that school officials and CAIR continue to coordinate together in secret.[17]

The lawsuit also uncovered clear indications that CAIR's pretext for proposing the program—a claim of widespread bullying of Muslim students—was a Trojan horse for smuggling Islamic indoctrination into the public schools. The school district's own statistics showed that, district-wide, there were only *two* recorded instances in which Muslim students were bullied, one in 2015 and another in 2016. For comparison, there were eleven instances of Jewish students being bullied during that time.

As the court filing states, "There are no programs [in the San Diego school system] promoting 'Jewish culture.' There are no lectures from priests on how to accommodate Catholic students during Lent. And there are no partnerships with Evangelical Christian activists. . . . [The district has placed its] power, prestige, and purse behind a single religion: Islam."[18]

Do you think the literature CAIR distributed to San Diego students honestly described how Islam was spread, century by century, through wars of conquest? Or do you think it's more likely that CAIR presented a whitewashed version of Islamic history?

CAIR's ultimate goal was made clear when Hanif Mohebi, executive director of CAIR-San Diego, told the *San Diego Union-Tribune* that the district's anti-bullying program should serve as a model for the rest of the nation. "If we do this right," he said, "San Diego Unified School District would be the leading school district in the nation to come up with a robust and beautiful anti-bully and anti-Islamophobic program."[19] In other words, today San Diego, tomorrow the nation.

This is cultural jihad at its most insidious—indoctrinating impressionable schoolchildren with one-sided propaganda provided by an Islamist organization with known ties to terrorist groups. And this stealth jihad is being carried out at taxpayer expense with the full compliance and complicity of San Diego school officials.

As this book goes to press, the lawsuit is unresolved and the San Diego school system continues to defend its CAIR-sponsored propaganda program. CAIR remains determined to impose state-sponsored schoolyard proselytizing on the nation. It is unacceptable for any American school system to be in partnership with CAIR—a group that both the FBI and the United

Arab Emirates agree is involved with the Muslim Brotherhood, terrorism, and jihad.

Political Muslim groups like CAIR seek to use the democratic process to do away with democracy and impose an Islamic theocracy. Political Muslims, who sound like moderate Muslims while quietly pursuing the same goals as militant Muslims, are the vanguard of the Third Jihad.

The emerging problem of Turkey

One of the most underreported hotspots of Third Jihad activity is the Republic of Turkey, which emerged from the ashes of the collapsed Ottoman Empire in 1920. Most Americans— even those who are well-informed about world events—pay little attention to Turkey. But I believe the Turks will prove to be a major adversary to the West as the Third Jihad unfolds.

Turkey is currently viewed as an American ally because of its membership in the North American Treaty Organization (NATO). After World War I, Turkish leaders restructured the nation as a parliamentary republic with a secular constitution. Turkey elected Mustafa Kemal as its first president. In 1934, the Turkish parliament honored Kemal with a special surname: Atatürk, which means "Father of the Turkish People."

For decades, the Republic of Turkey enjoyed close ties to America and other Western nations. There have been stresses and strains from time to time, but Turkey and the United States have been allies from the Cold War era right up through the War on Terror.

However, the spirit of cooperation between Turkey and the West has been slowly deteriorating since Recep Tayyip Erdoğan came to power, first as prime minister in 2003 and then as president in 2014. In 2016, Erdoğan cracked down on freedom of the press; today, one-third of all journalists imprisoned in the world are languishing in Turkish prisons.[20]

Erdoğan, an Islamist and a supporter of the Muslim Brotherhood, won reelection in 2018, becoming both head of state and head of the government. The Turkish people essentially voted away their secular democratic state and replaced it with something closer to the old Ottoman sultanate.

In his newly expanded role, Erdoğan has enormous influence, if not outright authority, over the Turkish legislature and courts. He has engineered a position much like that of Russia's Vladimir Putin, combining the apparent legitimacy of an elected president with the unrestrained power of an autocratic dictator. Erdoğan seems to be positioning Turkey for a return to what Islamists would view as the glory days of the old Ottoman Empire.

Islamists like Erdoğan understand that the key to controlling the future is to indoctrinate the next generation. So he has focused his attention on reshaping Turkey's educational system. According to Carlotta Gall of the *New York Times*, Erdoğan is firing tens of thousands of public school teachers and closing public schools, replacing them with fundamentalist Islamic schools. In 2012, while he was still prime minister, Erdoğan declared that his ultimate goal was to "raise a pious generation"—meaning a fundamentalist Muslim generation.[21]

There were 450 Islamic schools in Turkey when Erdoğan was first elected prime minister. Today there are 4,500 Islamic schools, all taxpayer funded and state controlled. Many Turkish public schools became religious schools without notifying parents. Students in those schools are required to be proficient in Arabic and Koran studies in order to graduate.[22]

Under Erdoğan, Turkey is taking a strong interventionist role in the Middle East, especially in Israel and the Palestinian territories. He has forged strong ties with Hamas, the Muslim Brotherhood-spawned Islamist group that regularly launches suicide bombings and rocket attacks into Israel. He also pours money and support into the Palestinian neighborhoods of East Jerusalem. As a result, Turkish flags now fly all around these neighborhoods and on the Temple Mount, the site of the al-Aqsa Mosque and the Dome of the Rock. Pro-Turkish demonstrations are regular occurrences on the Temple Mount.

Erdoğan has opened a Turkish cultural center in Jerusalem that offers concerts, lectures, and other cultural events. Turkey also has a seat on Jerusalem's Supreme Muslim Council. The Turkish government encourages its Muslim population to visit the Temple Mount in Jerusalem, to increase Turkey's influence on the city—and to stage demonstrations against the Israeli government.[23]

I fear that our own leaders, including President Donald Trump, do not fully appreciate the disastrous turn the Republic of Turkey has taken under President Erdoğan. During the July 2018 NATO Summit in Brussels, President Trump criticized European NATO nations for failing to meet goals set in 2014 to spend 2 percent of gross domestic product on defense.

One observer, CBS News contributor Ian Bremmer, said, "Trump was very frustrated; he wasn't getting commitments from other leaders to spend more. Many of them said, 'Well, we have to ask our parliaments. . . . We have a legal process.'"

Then Trump turned to President Erdoğan and said, "Except for Erdoğan over here. He does things the right way." Then Trump fist-bumped the Turkish president.[24]

I am grateful for the many accomplishments of the Trump Administration—increased support for the pro-life movement; the appointment of federal judges and Supreme Court justices who will uphold the Constitution; improved healthcare for veterans; a surging economy; progress on border security; reformed rules of engagement so our troops can succeed on the battlefield; and improved strategies toward Iran and Syria. But Mr. Trump needs to understand that the reason Recep Erdoğan doesn't have to consult with his parliament as other NATO leaders do is that he has established himself as an Ottoman-style sultan, an authoritarian Islamist dictator.

Just as an American president should not apologize for his country on foreign soil—as Barack Obama did—an American president should not share fist bumps with an Islamist dictator who promotes the Muslim Brotherhood, Hamas, and the Third Jihad.

The Republic of Turkey is on a dangerous path. Our leaders must learn to recognize an Islamist adversary when they see one.

8

THE THIRD JIHAD IN "EURABIA"

DURING THE SECOND WORLD WAR, in mid-July 1942, the Nazi occupation forces in Paris ordered the French police to arrest thousands of Jews and confine them at the Vélodrome d'Hiver, an indoor bicycle racing track and stadium near the Eiffel Tower. About thirteen thousand Jews—including more than four thousand children—were rounded up and held at the Vélodrome before being herded onto livestock railcars and transported to the Auschwitz death camp in Poland.

A nine-year-old Jewish-French girl named Mireille and her mother were on the list to be arrested, but Mireille escaped that fate because her mother had a Brazilian passport. Mother and daughter made their way to Portugal to await the end of the war. After the war, she and her mother moved back to Paris, among the few survivors left of the thirteen thousand Jews who were arrested and sent to the Vélodrome.

Miraculously, Mireille Knoll survived the Holocaust. She grew up, married a young Auschwitz survivor, and had children and grandchildren. After her husband passed away, Mireille continued to live in her Paris apartment, enjoying life and taking her grandchildren to parks, museums, and shows.

Mireille Knoll befriended a seven-year-old Arab-French boy named Yacine Mihoub. As the boy grew older, Mireille paid him to carry groceries for her. Yacine lived in the same apartment building as Mireille, and when she'd hear him skipping up the stairs, she'd open her door and chat with him. She kept in touch with Yacine after he was in his twenties—and according to Mireille's granddaughter, Keren Brosh, Grandma Mireille loved Yacine like a son.

Mireille rarely missed her favorite TV show, an American soap opera. She was probably watching that show on March 23, 2018, when she answered a knock on her door and found twenty-eight-year-old Yacine Mihoub standing in the hall. The young man entered Mireille Knoll's apartment, presumably at her invitation, and was later joined by twenty-one-year-old Alex Carrimbacus, a friend he had met in prison. At some point during the day, the two men pulled knives and attacked the eighty-five-year-old Holocaust survivor, stabbing her eleven times. At least one of those stab wounds proved fatal.

Carrimbacus later told police that Yacine shouted "Allahu Akbar!" (Allah is great!) as he murdered this woman who had never been anything but kind to him. The two young men then set the apartment on fire and left. The police arrested both of them within hours of the crime.[1]

Mireille's death was not just a random murder. It was specifically the killing of a Jew, carried out in the name of Allah. It was an act of jihad.

What would cause a young man to turn against a woman who had befriended him when he was seven years old? What would cause him to hate her so much that he could plunge a knife into her body again and again? What would cause him to shout "Allahu Akbar!" as he killed her? Such hate, fueled by religious passion, seems impossible to comprehend—yet it is all too common among Islamists.

The Third Jihad in France

In recent years, many Western nations have permitted a massive surge of Islamic immigration across their borders. Today, almost six million Muslims live in France, making Muslims the third-largest religious group in the country, after Roman Catholics and Protestants.[2]

According to Patrick Calvar, head of France's General Directorate for Internal Security, an estimated fifteen thousand of those Muslims in France are Salafists—jihad-minded Sunni Muslims whose radical, fundamentalist vison is to return civilization to the seventh century. "These Salafists," writes Italian journalist Giulio Meotti, "openly challenge France's way of life and do not make a secret of their willingness to overthrow the existing order in Europe through violent means, terror attacks, and physical intimidation."[3]

Yet it is political Islam, the so-called "quiet conquest" of Europe through gradual infiltration, that poses an even greater threat than violent jihad. The ambition of "moderate," political

Islam, Meotti writes, is clear: "changing French society. Slowly but surely."[4]

The Islamization of France has been so gradual, in fact, that few French citizens realized what a sizable presence radical Islam had established there, until the French Intifada (uprising) of 2005. Over a three-week period beginning on October 27, gangs of ethnic Arab youths rioted in the Parisian suburbs and in other French cities, torching schools, synagogues, post offices, fire stations, and warehouses. They fired on police and burned more than nine thousand cars and buses. Police arrested nearly twenty-eight hundred rioters.

A fifty-six-year-old disabled woman was trapped and severely burned inside a bus torched by rioting Muslim youths.[5] Two French men—a news photographer and a homeowner trying to extinguish a fire—were beaten to death by young thugs. Muslim rioters seemed bent on frightening French children by fire-bombing (at night) their nursery schools in Lille (near the Belgian border), Toulouse (in southern France), and Achères (about fifteen miles northwest of Paris).[6]

After the French Intifada, Libyan dictator Muammar Gadhafi (who was later killed in the 2011 Libyan uprising) said, "We have fifty million Muslims in Europe. There are signs that Allah will grant Islam victory in Europe—without swords, without guns, without conquest—[and] will turn it into a Muslim continent within a few decades."[7] The Muslim riots in France in 2005 inspired other riots across Europe—a Muslim youth riot in Brussels in September 2006; one in Amsterdam in 2007; another riot in France in November 2007; and a Muslim youth uprising in Sweden in May 2013.

Violent uprisings and terrorist attacks are part of a larger plan. They are intended to strike fear in the hearts of Westerners. The January 2015 shootings at the Paris office of the magazine *Charlie Hebdo*, a Jewish grocery store, and in the Paris suburb of Montrouge, killed seventeen and shocked the world. The November 2015 shootings and bombings at the Bataclan theater, and elsewhere in Paris, killed 130 and horrified the world. Violence instills fear—but violent jihad is not as effective at forcing change in Western society as cultural jihad, the quiet, gradual use of propaganda, legal manipulation, and social pressure to Islamicize Western civilization.

In July 2015, Dalil Boubakeur, the rector of the Grand Mosque in Paris, sparked outrage across France when he suggested that France should convert its empty, unused churches into mosques. One public opinion poll showed that only 5 percent of French citizens attend church weekly anyway, so why not? The director of the poll, Jérome Fourquet, noted that France has been "deeply de-Christianized since the 1960s."[8] It should surprise no one that, in France, Islam has rushed in to fill the void left by the retreat of Christianity.

The Third Jihad in Britain

Twenty-five-year-old Umar Haque was employed as an administrator and teacher at the Lantern of Knowledge Islamic School in east London, despite lacking any certification to teach. He also taught evening classes in a madrassa at the nearby Ripple Road Mosque. Haque taught Islamic studies to more than one hundred children, ages eleven through fourteen. As he taught the children, he was also recruiting "an army of child jihadists," according to *The Guardian*.[9]

Haque's methods were brutal. He showed the children graphic videos recorded by terrorists, depicting mangled, bloodied bodies; people tossed to their deaths from buildings; terrorists practicing killing techniques in training camps; and people being beheaded. Haque acted out the technique for severing a head with a knife—and threatened the children with beheading if they told anyone. He made them swear an oath of silence.

On another occasion, he showed the children a video in which the badly decomposed body of a young boy was exhumed from a grave. Then he told them the body was so gruesomely corrupted because angels had beaten the boy to death when he couldn't answer questions about the Koran. He also made the children compete against each other and wrestle with one another to prepare them as fighters.

After a March 2017 terrorist attack on Westminster Bridge, in which a jihadist plowed his car into a crowd of pedestrians near the Parliament building, Haque praised the terrorist. Then he role-played the attack with the children and told them they would someday carry out similar attacks. He planned to recruit three hundred young jihadists and unleash them in a frenzy of mass murder.

Police had become aware of Umar Haque's jihadist activities in April 2016, when he attempted to board an airliner for Istanbul, probably intending to join ISIS in Syria. Security officials revoked his passport and investigated his activities. Haque and three other young men were later arrested, and on March 2, 2018, he was convicted of conspiring to use guns and a car bomb to commit terror attacks on thirty high-profile targets, including Heathrow Airport, Parliament, the Queen's Guard, east London's Westfield shopping center, and various London news outlets. He was sentenced to life in prison.

Of the more than one hundred children Umar Haque tried to indoctrinate, none reported him to parents, teachers, or other authorities. His threats kept them silent. Even after Haque was arrested, most of the children were afraid to speak to the authorities. Only six testified against him at his trial.

One boy seemed to still be under the spell of Haque's brainwashing. "He has been training us, kind of," the boy said. "Apparently fighting is good. If you fight for the sake of Allah, on judgment day when you get judged for your good deeds and bad deeds, fighting is good." Thirty-five of Haque's students still receive long-term counseling and therapy.[10]

Ofsted—the Office for Standards in Education, Children's Services and Skills—had inspected the Lantern of Knowledge school during Haque's tenure. According to the inspectors' report, "The spiritual, moral, social, and cultural development of pupils is outstanding. They have an excellent understanding of the world around them and make a positive contribution to their community." Today, Ofsted is struggling to understand how their school inspectors came to that conclusion.[11]

Under the guise of moderate Islam, subversive agents of the Third Jihad (such as Umar Haque) are advancing an agenda that seeks to overthrow the governments and institutions of Western civilization. They will use any means to achieve their goals, including violence and murder. And they will, without conscience, destroy the lives of anyone, even innocent children.

An old proverb, said to be of Arabian origin, warns, "If the camel once gets his nose in the tent, his body will soon follow." In Great Britain, the nose of the camel called the Third Jihad is Sharia law. When the first Sharia council appeared in Britain in the 1980s, it was concerned primarily with granting divorces for Muslims in accordance with Islamic law. Gradually, over the years, the scope of Sharia council authority has grown.

Sharia councils became full-fledged arbitration tribunals under the 1996 Arbitration Act. If both parties agree in advance to the council's authority, its ruling is as binding as British law. Sheikh Faiz-ul-Aqtab Siddiqi of the Muslim Arbitration Tribunal has made it clear that Sharia is a separate but parallel legal system in Great Britain. "Because we follow the same process as any case of arbitration," he said, "our decisions are binding in English law. Unless our decisions are unreasonable, they are recognized by the High Court."[12] Siddiqi has also said that he expects Sharia courts to expand their jurisdiction into small criminal cases, not just civil. Once the Sharia courts begin adjudicating criminal matters according to Islamic law, the entire nose, head, and neck of the camel will be inside the tent.

In 2008, then archbishop of Canterbury (and head of the Anglican Church) Rowan Williams triggered a national uproar when he told an audience, "It seems inevitable that elements of the Muslim law, such as divorce proceedings, would be incorporated into British legislation."[13] Well, if the church and its influence on society are in full retreat, maybe it *is* inevitable that Sharia law will encroach on the British legal system. But if the church would be salt and light, as Jesus said, preserving and illuminating society with godly wisdom, then perhaps Western culture—and yes, British law—would stand firm against infiltration by Islamic law.

Under Sharia, women become second-class citizens, with far fewer rights than Western women have under Western law. For example, Faiz-ul-Aqtab Siddiqi and his Muslim Arbitration Tribunal decided to award the heirs of a deceased father unequal shares of the estate, based purely on gender. Each son received twice as much of the estate as each of the daughters. Under British law, the daughters and sons would have received equal shares.[14]

The current head of the Anglican Church, Archbishop of Canterbury Justin Welby, is an evangelical Christian who chooses to stand instead of retreat. As Welby himself explains:

> There has been, and remains, a demand for the introduction of those aspects of *Sharia* law that affect family and inheritance. . . .
>
> *Sharia*, which has a powerful and ancient cultural narrative of its own, deeply embedded in a system of faith and understanding of God, and thus especially powerful in forming identity, cannot become part of another narrative. It is either formative or different. Accepting it in part implies accepting its values around the nature of the human person, attitudes to outsiders, the revelation of God, and a basis for life in law, rather than grace, the formative word of Christian culture.[15]

In other words, Sharia descends from the Koran, a religious mind-set and a set of traditions completely unlike the Western mind-set and traditions of the common law legal system of England and Wales. British law descends from Judeo-Christian concepts of justice, Roman and Norman legal traditions, and the Magna Carta Libertatum (the Great Charter of Liberties) drafted by Archbishop of Canterbury Stephen Langton in 1215. We cannot graft Sharia onto English common law and expect it to produce justice any more than we could graft an apple tree branch onto a pine tree and expect it to produce pineapples.

Muslims view Sharia *not* as a series of governing rules, but as a spiritual path designed to draw Muslims closer to Allah. Sharia is all-encompassing, dealing not only with legal disputes and criminal behavior but also with prayer, rituals, blasphemy, and even the consumption of food. Sharia permits polygamy and often permits domestic violence against women, both of which are forbidden under English law. Matters of family law (marriage, divorce, property division, and child custody) are weighted heavily in favor of men and against women under Islamic law. Sharia, Archbishop Welby concludes, is simply incompatible with British law and should not be recognized as parallel to the British legal system.[16]

Another nonviolent form of jihad used by Islamists in Great Britain is a campaign of intimidation, bullying, and insult. Islamists use the rights and freedoms afforded them by British law in their efforts to do away with those very rights and freedoms.

For example, the little town of Royal Wootton Bassett, seventy miles west of London, gained fame for its patriotic processions, welcoming home Britain's fallen soldiers from the wars in Iraq and Afghanistan. Beginning in 2007, vehicles bearing flag-draped coffins passed through town on their way from RAF Lyneham airbase to Oxford. At first, only a small group of veterans from the local Royal British Legion showed up to salute.

In time, the numbers of townspeople along the route grew to more than a thousand.

Then Islamist protesters began to show up, carrying signs and shouting slogans, calling the fallen soldiers "murderers" and "baby killers." During one such protest, police arrested five British Muslim men, who were later convicted of harassment and using insulting language in their protests. The slap-on-the-wrist sentence: court costs and two years' probation. The unrepentant Islamist defendants refused to stand in court—a show of disrespect for British legal authority—and later stood outside the courthouse waving a sign that read, "Islam will dominate! Freedom can go to hell."[17]

The Islamists' contempt for freedom speaks volumes about the gulf between Western culture and the Islamist worldview, which *welcomes* and *rejoices in* the oppression found in a theocratic Islamic state. The only use the Islamists have for freedom is to use it against us and bring about a totalitarian caliphate.

And let's not leave Vladimir Putin and the Russian Federation out of this picture. Now-retired Air Force General Philip M. Breedlove was Supreme Allied Commander Europe for NATO from 2013 to 2016. In March 2016, he testified before the Senate Armed Services Committee that Russia and Syria were bombing civilians as part of a deliberate attempt to explode the refugee crisis and cause terrified Syrians to flee to Europe. Putin, Breedlove said, was seeking to "weaponize migration"— to turn Syrian immigrants into a weapon of mass destabilization to wreck the European culture, economy, and political system.[18]

Breedlove pointed to the Syrian and Russian use of "barrel bombs" in populated areas as proof of his contention. Barrel bombs are metal containers filled with explosives, shrapnel, flammable oil, and deadly chemicals. Dropped from helicopters or airplanes, they are hopelessly inaccurate and serve no military purpose. Their only use is to kill, maim, and terrify civilians.

Russian and Syrian forces, said Breedlove, have also targeted hospitals and other civilian centers. As a result, ten times as many refugees surged north from Syria into Turkey in 2016 as in 2015, which itself had been a record year for refugees. From Turkey, these asylum seekers crossed the Aegean Sea into Europe—usually with criminals and terrorists traveling among them.[19]

António Guterres, former High Commissioner for Refugees at the United Nations, said that ISIS was pursuing the same strategy of spreading terror and swelling the refugee crisis in order to divide Europe. The strategy, he said, "is not only to set Europeans against refugees, but within Europe, to set citizen against citizen within communities, community against community within countries, and country against country in the [European] Union."[20]

Political Islam has a plan for France, Great Britain—for all of Europe, and for the United States as well. It's the same plan that political Islam has had since the seventh century: conquest and unconditional surrender to the global caliphate. One British-based Islamist group that is pursuing this goal is Al-Muhajiroun (the Emigrants). After being banned by the British government, the group has resurfaced under an assortment of names. (Islam4UK, the Saved Sect, the Sharia Project, and the Islamic Dawah Association are believed to be among its aliases.)

Soon after the 9/11 attacks in 2001, one of the group's

leaders, Omar Bakri Mohammed, said, "We would not carry out terrorist activity ourselves, but we endorse the use of violence. Bin Laden is a hero to all Muslims. . . . I want Britain to become an Islamic state. I want to see the flag of Islam raised in 10 Downing Street."[21]

Political Islam has issued a challenge to our entire civilization. We can laugh off those words or shrug them off, or we can work as hard to strengthen our civilization as the Islamists are working to destroy it.

Transforming Europe into Eurabia

The planned Islamic conquest of Europe by the Ottoman Empire was stopped in its tracks on September 12, 1683, outside the gates of Vienna. That's the day the forces of King John III Sobieski of Poland poured out of the Vienna Woods, scattering and slaughtering the Ottoman army. The Islamists never again threatened a takeover of Europe.

Until now.

In 2006, Italian journalist Oriana Fallaci wrote in *The Force of Reason* that Europe is already "a colony of Islam and Italy an outpost of that province, a stronghold of that colony. . . . In each one of our cities there is a second city, a state within the state, a government within the government. A Muslim city, a city ruled by the Koran. An Islamic expansionism's stage. The expansionism that no one has ever managed to overcome. No one. Not even the armies of Napoleon."[22]

Islam's "most coveted prey," she wrote, "has always been Europe, the Christian world."[23] Fallaci went on to recount the history of Islamic conquests: In 635, three years after

Muhammad's death, the armies of Islam invaded Christian Syria and Christian Palestine. In 638, Islamists conquered Jerusalem. In 640, they conquered Persia, Armenia, and Mesopotamia and invaded Christian Egypt and Christian North Africa. In 711, they invaded Christian Spain.

Fallaci suggested we should study "the stories of the burned convents and monasteries, of the profaned churches, of the raped nuns, of the Christian or Jewish women abducted to be locked away in their harems . . . [and] the crucifixions of Córdoba, the hangings of Granada, the beheadings of Toledo and Barcelona, of Seville and Zamora."[24]

A lifelong atheist, Oriana Fallaci was an unlikely defender of Christianity. Abrasive and unpredictable, she interviewed some of the world's greatest leaders and dictators. Her interview with unrepentant terrorist Yasser Arafat, then head of the Palestine Liberation Organization, was angry and contentious. For her interview with Ayatollah Khomeini, Iran's revolutionary leader, she agreed to wear a robe-like chador over her blouse and skirt—then tore off the chador in the ayatollah's presence to show him what she thought of Islam's oppression of women.

A chain smoker, Fallaci was diagnosed with lung cancer in the mid-1990s. After the 9/11 terror attacks, she wrote several books warning of the Islamist threat to Western civilization. Muslim pressure groups mounted an intense effort to silence her. An array of Muslim advocacy groups in Switzerland filed multiple lawsuits against her, and the Swiss courts did their best to bully her into submission. At one time, the Swiss government petitioned the Italian government to extradite Fallaci so that she could stand trial.

Why was Switzerland, among all the nations of Europe, so intent on prosecuting Fallaci for publishing the truth about political Islam? "Switzerland [is] where the sons of Allah are now more numerous and more arrogant than at Mecca," she explained. "And where in 1995 the Article 261b of the Criminal Code was written for their benefit. (The Article allows a Muslim immigrant to win any ideological or private lawsuit by invoking religious racism and racial discrimination.)"[25]

Islamist groups also sued Fallaci in the French courts, and an Italian judge indicted her on charges of xenophobia—an indictment that, because of European Union arrest warrant regulations, made the entire continent of Europe unsafe for her. She spent the final years of her life in the United States, dying of cancer but safe from the predatory civil and criminal lawsuits that had been filed against her—a reminder of why First Amendment freedom of speech is so important to Americans.

In 2005, Fallaci met secretly with Pope Benedict XVI. Though she never revealed what they discussed, she did begin calling herself a "Christian atheist" in the final years of her life. In late 2006, she returned to her hometown of Florence, Italy, knowing she would die before the Italian courts could cause her any more harm. She passed away ten days after arriving home, on September 15, 2006.[26]

I certainly don't agree with everything Oriana Fallaci did, said, or wrote. I tell her story to illustrate what those who speak the truth about political Islam are up against. The Islamists will use the laws and courts of Western nations to destroy anyone who speaks up—and the courts will eagerly assist in the destruction of the truth tellers. The legal systems of Europe and America are aiding and abetting the destruction of Western civilization.

Europe is gradually transforming into *Eurabia*—a term coined by Bat Ye'or (the pen name of historian Gisèle Littman). As Christianity has been dying a slow death in Europe and ancient churches have been turned into museums and even mosques, Islam has been rushing in to fill the spiritual vacuum. Europe is becoming—as Oriana Fallaci predicted—a staging area for global jihad.

Some analysts worry that the culture clash between Westerners and inflooding Muslims could erupt into open, violent warfare. I don't think so. War breaks out when an aggressor tries to conquer what a defender wishes to defend. What does Europe have that is worth defending? The Christian faith and traditions? Christian history and culture? No. If Europe had prized its history as the birthplace of the Roman Church and the Protestant Reformations, European churches would not now be dark and empty.

Unless revival comes to Europe, that continent will probably be conquered by Islam—not through armed conflict, but through patient, gradual cultural jihad. At some point, while no one is noticing or caring, Europe will cease to be free and democratic. Western civilization in Europe will turn to dust and blow away.

Though the Islamic warriors of the Third Jihad will use violence when they have to, the Third Jihad will largely be a quiet, gradual conquest. It will be carried out through Western media, the Western legal system, and Western governments. Anyone who speaks out against the Islamization of Europe will be silenced. The people of Europe won't even know they have surrendered to political Islam until it is too late.

9

COULD IT HAPPEN HERE?

ON TUESDAY MORNING, SEPTEMBER 11, 2001, United Airlines Flight 175 took off from Logan International Airport in Boston, bound for Los Angeles. Half an hour after takeoff, five al-Qaeda terrorists seized control of the Boeing 767, overpowering the pilot and first officer. The terrorists flew the aircraft to New York, where the north tower of the World Trade Center was already burning, struck seventeen minutes earlier by another hijacked airliner.

At 9:03 a.m., United Flight 175 crashed into the south tower, killing all sixty-five people aboard, along with an unknown number of occupants of the building. As fire and smoke billowed into the air, debris shot out of the opposite side of the south tower and rained down on the streets and buildings below. Parts of United Flight 175's landing gear, fuselage, and engine struck the roof of a five-story building at 45-47 Park Place, smashing through two floors and shattering steel floor beams.

The Park Place building, which had been built a few years before the start of the Civil War, stood empty for years after the 9/11 attacks. Finally, in July 2009, an Egyptian-American real estate developer purchased the property. Soon afterward, an Egyptian-American Muslim cleric, Imam Feisal Abdul Rauf, announced plans to develop the site into a thirteen-story Islamic community center to "promote dialogue" between Islam and other faiths.

Opposition to the project, especially from families affected by 9/11, was immediate and impassioned. The developers called the project Park51, Rauf called it Cordoba House, but opponents called it the Ground Zero mosque.

Though Imam Rauf claims to be a moderate Muslim and has condemned the 9/11 attacks, he has also said that 9/11 was an understandable—even inevitable—Islamic reaction to American foreign policy. In a CBS *60 Minutes* interview in late September 2001, Rauf explained his views.

"I wouldn't say that the United States deserved what happened," he said, "but United States' policies were an accessory to the crime that happened."

When questioned further about this, he added, "We [the USA] have been an accessory to a lot of—of innocent lives dying in the world. In fact, it—in the most direct sense, Osama bin Laden is made in the USA."[1]

In 2008, Rauf published a book called *What's Right with Islam Is What's Right with America*. Columnist Andrew McCarthy, a former Assistant United States Attorney who has won convictions against terrorists, investigated Rauf's book and found it was originally published under a different title in Malaysia: *A Call to Prayer from the World Trade Center Rubble: Islamic Dawa in the Heart of America Post-9/11*. The American edition was copublished by two Islamist organizations with ties to the Muslim Brotherhood.

What does "Islamic dawa" mean? McCarthy explains:

Dawa, whether done from the rubble of the World Trade Center or elsewhere, is the missionary work by which Islam is spread. . . .

Scholar Robert Spencer incisively refers to *dawa* practices as "stealth jihad," the advancement of the sharia agenda through means other than violence and agents other than terrorists. These include extortion, cultivation of sympathizers in the media and the universities, exploitation of our legal system and tradition of religious liberty, infiltration of our political system, and fundraising. This is why Yusuf Qaradawi, the spiritual leader of the Muslim Brotherhood and the world's most influential Islamic cleric, boldly promises that Islam will "conquer America" and "conquer Europe" through *dawa*.[2]

So, while the title of the American edition of Imam Rauf's book proclaims *solidarity* between America and Islam, the title of the original Malaysian edition claims the rubble of 9/11 as ground zero for a new mission to Islamicize America. Rauf's Cordoba House project played a key role in his vision for dawa in America.

Planting the flag at Ground Zero

The proposed location for Cordoba House—which has still yet to be built and may never be—is not merely two blocks from Ground Zero. To the Islamists, it is *part* of Ground Zero.

Fragments of the aircraft used in the attack caused structural damage to the original building on the site. Because of that damage, Muslim real estate developers purchased the site at an advantageous price, and Imam Rauf planned to use the site to build an Islamic house of worship.

The symbolism of what came to be known as the Ground Zero mosque was apparently lost on politicians (such as New York mayor Michael Bloomberg and President Barack Obama) who supported Imam Rauf's plan to build an Islamic center there. But the symbolism was not lost on millions of Muslims around the world who know that whenever Islamic armies conquer a city, the conquerors establish a mosque there. Establishing a mosque on conquered land is like planting the flag of Islam.

Why did Rauf call his project Cordoba House? The city of Córdoba in the Andalusia region of southern Spain has become, for some historians, a symbol of peaceful coexistence between the world's great religions. Many academics embrace a theory called *La Convivencia*, meaning "the coexistence." They claim that, after the Umayyad Islamic conquest of Spain in the early eighth century, Muslims, Christians, and Jews in Córdoba lived together in a golden age of tolerance and harmony.[3] But life in Muslim-occupied Córdoba was hardly a "golden age" for Christians and Jews. In fact, the Córdoba-born Muslim historian Ibn Hazm proudly proclaimed the Umayyads to be "the most afflicting to the enemies of God"[4]—by which he meant Christians and Jews.

Dario Fernández-Morera, professor of medieval Spanish culture at Northwestern University, writes, "The celebrated Umayyads actually elevated religious and political persecutions, inquisitions, beheadings, impalings, and crucifixions to heights unequaled by any other set of rulers before or after in Spain."[5] Fernández-Morera adds that Abd al-Rahman I, the founder of the Umayyad dynasty, ordered the destruction of the Catholic Basilica of Saint Vincent so that the Mezquita (Great Mosque) of Córdoba could be built on its ruins—a symbol of Muslim conquest of Christian land.

Córdoba-born Jewish philosopher Moses Maimonides fled Córdoba after a new Muslim dynasty, the Almohads, came to power in 1148 and began forcing Jews and Christians to convert to Islam. Confronted with a choice of converting, losing his head, or fleeing into exile, Maimonides chose exile. In his *Letter to the Jews of Yemen*, Maimonides wrote of the intense persecution in Córdoba and across the Muslim world: "Dear brothers, because of our many sins Hashem ["the Name," which is a reference to God] has cast us among this nation, the Arabs, who are treating us badly. They pass laws designed to cause us distress and make us despised. The Torah foretold: 'Our enemies will judge us' (Devarim 32:31). Never has there been a nation that hated, humiliated, and loathed us as much as this one."[6]

When Imam Rauf proposed to name his Ground Zero Islamic center after Córdoba, he wanted Western audiences to think of a golden age of interfaith tolerance. But Islamic audiences would know that Córdoba symbolized conquest. That's why, of all the properties Imam Rauf could have chosen for his Islamic center, the only building he wanted was the one damaged by aircraft debris in the 9/11 attack. The damaged building symbolized American land conquered in war by Muslim martyrs.

It's a pattern as old as Islam itself: conquer land and establish a mosque there. In 630, Muhammad led a legion of militant followers from Medina to Mecca. There the first army of Islam slaughtered the "unbelievers" and "polytheists" of that city, destroying their idols. The Muslims converted the cube-shaped Kaaba from a temple of the Arab god Hubal to the holiest site of Islam.

In 638, Muslim warriors under Umar ibn al-Khattab conquered Jerusalem. The Umayyad Dynasty built the Dome of the Rock on the Temple Mount, obliterating the most sacred site of Judaism. The gleaming Dome of the Rock dominates Jerusalem's skyline to this day.

In 705, the Umayyad Dynasty converted the Church of John the Baptist into the Great Mosque of Damascus.

In 1453, the Ottomans under Mehmed the Conqueror captured Constantinople and immediately converted the thousand-year-old Orthodox church called the Hagia Sophia into a huge mosque.

In the Muslim mind, the construction of a mosque gives Islam a permanent, irrevocable claim to the site. Thereafter, that land becomes Muslim land. Can there be any doubt about the true purpose of Cordoba House? It follows the ancient pattern of Islamic conquest. Yet anyone who criticized the Cordoba House initiative was branded an Islamophobe.

I believe it's far better to be falsely accused of Islamophobia than to support a symbol of Islamic conquest and declare to the world, "We submit to Islamic rule." Yet that is what our government has said to the world in many ways. Political Islam is winning the battle without even raising the sword.

The goal of dawa

There are millions of moderate, tolerant Muslims in the world—but not all Muslims who claim to be moderate truly are. Some put on a pretense of moderation while pursuing cultural jihad. In Islam, there is an Arabic term—*taqiya*—for the practice of obscuring the truth to protect oneself or the Islamic religion. *Taqiya* literally means "prudence in fear." A related Arabic term *kitmān* means "covering the truth," the act of misleading through maintaining silence or neglecting to speak the truth.

In previous centuries, Muslims employed taqiya to avoid being persecuted. Increasingly, however, Muslim leaders employ taqiya to mislead political opponents and advance an Islamist agenda. One such leader is Tariq Ramadan, a Swiss academic, who has taught at Oxford and at universities in Qatar, Morocco, and Japan.

In an article written for the Middle East Media Research Institute, Aluma Dankowitz cites the work of French journalist Caroline Fourest, author of the book *Frère Tariq* (*Brother Tariq*) published in 2004:

> Fourest examines Ramadan's sophisticated message, pointing out that he conveys one message to a Muslim audience and a different message to the larger public, and that sometimes he is even capable

of addressing both audiences simultaneously and conveying a different message to each.[7]

In the words of Egyptian journalist Adel Guindy, "Doublespeak is the key to understanding Tariq Ramadan."[8] Aluma Dankowitz adds: "In his audio recording *Islam and the West*, Ramadan sets out his strategy as follows: 'I must speak in a way that is appropriate for the ear hearing me . . . yet faithful to the religious sources of authority.' He advises his listeners to adopt a cautious media strategy: 'We must know how to speak to those who do not share our history.'"[9] That is the doublespeak of taqiya.

When Ramadan was asked whether he defended terrorism or condemned it, he took both sides, saying, "Of course we condemn terrorism . . . but we support the resistance."[10] The resistance, of course, refers to terrorists. On another occasion, a reporter asked Ramadan his views on the murder of an eight-year-old Israeli boy by Palestinian Muslims. Again, he took both sides: "This deed in and of itself is worthy of condemnation, but it is understandable under present circumstances. . . . It is forbidden to attack civilians, but the US government policy leaves the Palestinians no other choice."[11]

Islamists such as Tariq Ramadan and Imam Rauf have developed the fine art of looking and sounding moderate and tolerant, so as to ingratiate themselves with leftist, secularist political leaders. By making friends in Western social, academic, entertainment, and political circles, Islamists can advance their agenda without alarming the secular left. They believe in coexisting with Western constitutional democracies—for now. Patience is their strategy, and their goal is dawa—injecting Islam into Western society through stealth missionary efforts. It is jihad with a warm handshake, conquest with an insincere smile.

I recently came across a subtle and deceptive example of Islamic dawa aimed at converting biblically unaware (and unwary) Christians to Islam. It's a tract, looking very much like a Christian tract. The word *JESUS* dominates the front panel in large capital letters: "JESUS—A PROPHET OF GOD—MUSLIMS ♥ JESUS." A tagline at the bottom reads, "Gain Peace Through Islam!"

If your mind has been well-saturated by the Word of God, this tract will not fool you for a moment. But as you read through it and observe its sly arguments, you can almost hear the sinister voice of the serpent of Eden lurking behind the reasonable sounding words:

> Some Christians claim that "Jesus is God" or part of a trinity—that he is the incarnation of God on earth, and that God took on a human form. However, according to the Bible, Jesus was born, ate, slept, prayed, and had limited knowledge—all attributes not befitting God. God has attributes of perfection whereas Man is the opposite. How can anything be two complete opposites simultaneously?
>
> Islam teaches that God is *always* perfect. To believe that God became a man is to claim that God is or was (at some point in time) imperfect. A Christian must ask him/herself, does the idea of a god who was once a weak, helpless child, one who could not survive without food, drink, or sleep, be the same Almighty God described in the Old Testament? Surely not.

Notice this phrase in the second sentence: "However, according to the Bible . . ." As when the devil tempted Jesus in the wilderness, the publishers of this tract invoke God's Word in an attempt to deceive. After saying, "According to the Bible," they argue purely from human reasoning. If it were actually "according to the Bible," wouldn't they quote what Jesus declares about himself in the Bible?

In John 10:30, Jesus says, "I and the Father are one." Hearing this, some of the people picked up stones, intending to execute Jesus on the spot. When Jesus asked them why they wanted to kill him, they replied, "For blasphemy, because you, a mere man, claim to be God."[12]

In John 14, Jesus also says, "I am the way and the truth and the life. No one comes to the Father except through me. . . . Anyone who has seen me has seen the Father."[13] Clearly, *according to the Bible,* Jesus claimed to be God.

In his various letters, the apostle Paul repeatedly affirms that Jesus is God. I'll quote just one, for example: "In Christ all the fullness of the Deity lives in bodily form."[14]

The tract states: "Some Christians claim that 'Jesus is God' or a part of a trinity." No, this is not what "some Christians claim." This is the truth that Jesus himself revealed: "Go and make disciples of all nations, baptizing them in the name of the Father and of the Son and of the Holy Spirit."[15]

If the producers of this Muslim tract were intellectually honest, they would not claim to argue "according to the Bible" while hiding and distorting what the Bible really says. There are many more slyly deceptive lies in this tract, but the closing lie is especially insidious:

Islam teaches that God is the All-Just and All-Merciful and does
not need to sacrifice himself to forgive sins nor is anyone "born
into sin." God judges everyone based on their own deeds and
everyone is accountable for their own actions. . . . Acknowledging
Jesus as a Prophet of God and becoming a Muslim does not mean
changing or losing your Christian identity. It is about going back
to the original and pure teachings of Jesus.

It's interesting that this tract doesn't dare to quote any of "the
original and pure teachings of Jesus" from the Bible. For as
Jesus said of himself, "I am the good shepherd . . . and I lay
down my life for the sheep."[16] He also said, "This is my blood
of the covenant, which is poured out for many for the forgiveness of sins."[17] From this brief examination of a Muslim tract
directed at gullible Christians, you can easily see the deliberate
dishonesty of Islamic dawa.

Author, scholar, and activist Ayaan Hirsi Ali has a deep
understanding of the threat posed by political Islam and dawa
in Western nations. Born in Somalia, the daughter of a promi-
nent Somali politician, Hirsi Ali was once a devout Muslim but
is now one of the world's leading critics of Islam. She advocates
the liberation of Muslim women and ending all forced marriages, child marriages, female genital mutilation, and honor
violence in Muslim families. In a 2017 article she wrote for
The Federalist, Hirsi Ali describes the Muslim practice of dawa:

The term "dawa" refers to activities carried out by Islamists
to win adherents and enlist them in a campaign to impose
sharia law on all societies. Dawa is not the Islamic equivalent

of religious proselytizing, although it is often disguised as such by blending humanitarian activities with subversive political activities.

Dawa as practiced by Islamists employs a wide range of mechanisms to advance the goal of imposing Islamic law (sharia) on society. This includes proselytization, but extends beyond that. In Western countries, dawa aims both to convert non-Muslims to political Islam and to bring about more extreme views among existing Muslims. The ultimate goal of dawa is to destroy the political institutions of a free society and replace them with strict sharia. Islamists rely on both violent and nonviolent means to achieve their objectives. . . .

[Dawa] is subversion from within, the use of religious freedom in order to undermine that very freedom.[18]

In her youth, Ayaan Hirsi Ali was passionate about her Muslim beliefs. Her grandmother had arranged for her to undergo the excruciating rite of female circumcision when she was five. Throughout her childhood, she was steeped in the Koran and says she lived "for the Book, by the Book." During her youth, Hirsi Ali's family lived for a while in Mecca. In her book *Heretic: Why Islam Needs a Reformation Now*, she recalls that it was in Mecca that she first learned what the strict application of Sharia law looked and sounded like:

In the public squares, every Friday, after the ritual prayers, men were beheaded or flogged, women were stoned, and thieves had their hands cut off amid great spurts of blood. The rhythm of chanted prayers was replaced by the reverberation of metal blades slicing through flesh and hitting stone. My brother—who, unlike me, was allowed to witness these punishments—used the nickname "Chop-Chop Square" for the one closest to us. We never questioned the ferocity of the punishments.[19]

As a teenager, Hirsi Ali embraced everything political Islam stood for, including jihad and the desire to see Sharia law obeyed everywhere by everyone. She supported the Islamist goals of the Muslim Brotherhood, and she agreed with the fatwa calling for the death of author Salman Rushdie for his portrayal of Muhammad in his novel *The Satanic Verses*. She even accepted her status as a marginalized woman in an oppressive Muslim society and was proud to wear the black hijab that covered her from head to foot.

When Hirsi Ali was twenty-two and living with her family in Kenya, a Somali man who was living in Canada came to Nairobi to find a bride. He called on Hirsi Ali's father, and the two men talked for about ten minutes. By the end of the conversation, Ayaan Hirsi Ali was engaged to a man she had never met. When she was introduced to her fiancé, the man immediately told her he intended to have six sons with her. After her first meeting with her husband-to-be, Hirsi Ali told her father she didn't want to marry the man. He replied that the date was set, and that was that. The wedding would take place in Canada.

A few months later, Hirsi Ali boarded a flight from Nairobi to Düsseldorf, Germany, where she was to change planes and fly to Canada. Instead, she walked around Düsseldorf, thinking about her future, and found herself taking a train to Amsterdam.

In the Netherlands, she claimed to be an asylum seeker fleeing the Somali civil war.

Hirsi Ali remained in the Netherlands, made many European friends, and studied the writers and philosophers of the Enlightenment era. At first, she felt guilty about fleeing from her family, her culture, and her arranged marriage. In her heart, she was still a Muslim.

"Even in running away from my arranged marriage," she later recalled, "I believed that Sharia punishments would follow me because that was the rule in my own community."[20]

Over time, however, Hirsi Ali became increasingly comfortable with the freedom she experienced in the Netherlands. She began to question her Islamic beliefs, and before long, she declared herself an atheist.

In 2004, Hirsi Ali collaborated with writer-filmmaker Theo van Gogh on a ten-minute film called *Submission*, about the oppression of women under Islam. The film aired on Dutch public TV in August. In November, a Moroccan-Dutch Islamist ambushed van Gogh while he rode his bicycle along the street in broad daylight. The attacker shot the filmmaker eight times with a handgun, then stabbed and nearly beheaded him. Before fleeing, the attacker pinned a note to van Gogh's body containing death threats against Hirsi Ali.

After the attack on Theo van Gogh, Hirsi Ali moved to the United States, where she is now a fellow with the Hoover Institution at Stanford University. When India-born British journalist Tunku Varadarajan interviewed Hirsi Ali in 2017 for *The Wall Street Journal*, he reflected, "I'm talking to a woman with multiple fatwas on her head, someone who has a greater chance of meeting a violent end than anyone I've met."[21] Paradoxically, the harshest criticism she receives comes from the secular left. She explains:

> For expressing the idea that Islamic violence is rooted not in social, economic, or political conditions—or even in theological error—but rather in the foundational texts of Islam itself, I have been denounced as a bigot and an "Islamophobe." I have been silenced, shunned, and shamed. In effect, I have been deemed to be a heretic, not just by Muslims—for whom I am already an apostate—but by some Western liberals as well, whose multicultural sensibilities are offended by such "insensitive" pronouncements. . . .
>
> Today, it seems, speaking the truth about Islam is a crime. "Hate speech" is the modern term for heresy. And in the present atmosphere, anything that makes Muslims feel uncomfortable is branded as "hate."[22]

Hirsi Ali understands better than most Westerners the goals of the Islamists because she was raised as an Islamist, she was steeped in Islamism and Sharia, and she understands the thinking that underlies jihad and dawa. America's war on terror, she says, has failed because *terror* is not an enemy. Our enemy in the Third Jihad is the Islamist ideology.

Her argument makes sense. When you fight a war, you almost always fight an ideology. In World War II, the Allies fought three distinct ideologies—German Nazism, Italian fascism, and Japanese imperialism. During the Cold War, our ideological enemy was Soviet communism. Why, then, aren't we fighting the Islamist ideology today? Why are we focusing all our attention on violent acts of terrorism instead of the underlying cause of Islamism? We have been fighting the wrong war, and that's why we're losing.

The Islamists know that Westerners do not grasp the Third Jihad. They understand that while we are playing Whac-A-Mole with terrorists, they are winning the *real* war by waging stealth jihad and dawa. They take advantage of the protections afforded by free societies to carry on their so-called missionary activity, worming their way into the good graces of government agencies and left-wing organizations by posing as moderate Muslims.

Ayaan Hirsi Ali lists a number of supposedly moderate Muslim organizations that, in her view, engage in Islamist dawa: the Council on American-Islamic Relations (CAIR), the Muslim Public Affairs Council (MPAC), the Islamic Society of North America (ISNA), the International Institute of Islamic Thought (IIIT), and the Islamic Society of Boston. These groups seek to discredit genuinely moderate Muslim reformers while elevating the Muslim Brotherhood and similar hard-line Islamist groups as the true representatives of all Muslims.

These Islamist groups also take advantage of the obsession with political correctness of secular progressives, using terms such as *inclusion, multiculturalism, coexistence,* and *tolerance* to shame and intimidate the secular left into accepting Islamist demands. For example, the organizers of the January 2017 Women's March on Washington chose as their co-chair an Islamist, Linda Sarsour (hailed by President Obama as "a champion of change"). Leftists seem blissfully unconcerned that

Sarsour openly advocates Sharia law in America, even though Sharia is incompatible with inclusion, tolerance, democracy, First Amendment freedom, gender equality, and LGBT rights—all causes that liberals claim to support.

Hirsi Ali also notes that the Islamists study Western society to find "points of vulnerability"—segments of the population that are especially likely to be swayed by the Islamist message. She says that Islamists target African-American men in prisons and infiltrate radical activist movements such as Black Lives Matter. Islamist groups also infiltrate and put pressure on public schools, charter schools, and private schools, dictating what schools may and may not say about Islam. These groups suggest "guidelines" for how politicians and journalists should talk and write about Islam—and anyone who violates the Islamists' guidelines is likely to be branded an Islamophobe. By controlling the words we can use when talking about Islam, the Islamists seek to control how we think.

It's time to wake up and recognize dawa for what it is. Violent Islamists took down the World Trade Center towers and attacked the Pentagon—but nonviolent Islamists are taking down our culture and our educational system. As Ayaan Hirsi Ali warns, dawa is simply jihad by other means.

"Nonviolent and violent Islamists differ only on tactics," she writes. "They share the same goal, which is to establish an unfree society ruled by strict Sharia law."[23]

Terrorism is not the enemy. Terrorism is a *tactic*. The real enemy is Islamist ideology. While we continue to battle violent jihad at home and abroad, we need to battle Islamist ideology as well. Whether we choose to be at war with the Islamists, they are at war with us and our children and grandchildren. Whether we choose to accept it or not, we and our families are on the front lines, facing the Third Jihad.

Islamists and the First Amendment

The American government was established to protect the rights and freedoms of all Americans. The purpose of government in the minds of Islamists is diametrically opposed to the purpose of government under the American Constitution. The Islamists are working patiently to transform government into the enforcement arm of political Islam.

The founding fathers had witnessed the oppression and injustice that results when church power and state power are wedded. They wanted nothing to do with establishing a theocracy in America. That's why the opening line of the First Amendment to the Constitution reads, "Congress shall make no law respecting an establishment of religion."

On January 1, 1802, President Thomas Jefferson wrote a letter to the Danbury Baptist Association, assuring Baptists in Connecticut that the Constitution views religion as "a matter which lies solely between Man & his God," and that the First Amendment established "a wall of separation between Church & State."[24] When Jefferson invented the phrase "separation of church and state," he meant, of course, that the government is forbidden to meddle in the affairs of the church. He did not mean (as so many secular leftists have lately claimed) that Christians and churches are not allowed to have any influence on the government.

The founding fathers made sure that the government would

not establish a state church, nor would the government interfere with the free exercise of religion. This is because the framers of the Constitution held a Judeo-Christian worldview. They understood that the Christian faith is not spread by force, but by an invitation to freely receive the gospel. No one who follows the teachings of Jesus Christ would ever hold a sword to the throat of another human being and say, "Convert or die." Free will is a core value of Christianity.

By contrast, the core value of Islam is not freedom but *surrender*, which is what the word *Islam* means. Islamists believe that Islam is more than a mere religion—rather, it's a comprehensive religious and political system that must exercise the full power of the state, meaning that all other peoples and religions must surrender to Islam. Fundamentalist, political Islam is codified intolerance for all other religions and political systems. This poses a troubling question for those of us who believe in the American Constitution and the First Amendment: Is a religious system that is determined to do away with our constitutional freedoms entitled to protection under the free exercise clause of the Constitution?

The answer is *yes*. In America, Muslims—including fundamentalist, political, Islamist Muslims—have a constitutional right to the free exercise of their religion, the right of free speech, and the right of freedom of the press. Under the First Amendment, American Muslims are free to preach their religion and advocate for their political views. Muslims are even free, under the Constitution, to proclaim that Sharia law should replace the Constitution.

Still, the Supreme Court has held that even the free exercise clause of the First Amendment has its limits. In Reynolds v. United States (1878), the high court ruled that the Mormon practice of polygamy was not protected by the First Amendment. The court reasoned that if polygamy were allowed, another religion might come along and claim that human sacrifice was protected under the free exercise clause. In Bob Jones University v. United States (1983), the high court ruled that the IRS could revoke the tax-exempt status of the university because of its racial discrimination policies (at that time, BJU prohibited interracial dating and interracial marriage).

The First Amendment gives all religions, including Islam, the right to believe and say whatever they want. And the First Amendment gives Christians the right to speak out and challenge the Islamists who are trying to subvert our Constitution.

But the First Amendment doesn't protect all religious *practices*. Islamists can say, "The Constitution should be replaced by Sharia law," but they are not permitted to take action to overthrow the government and force that belief on all Americans. Some Muslim sects and communities permit polygamy, wife-beating, honor killings, beheadings, stonings, and female genital mutilation—but the First Amendment does not protect such practices. As with all religions in America, the free exercise of Islam stops at the point where it would infringe on the life, rights, and freedoms of other individuals and religions.

Religious freedom in America is a delicate constitutional balancing act. That's why it's so important to have judges at every level—and especially on the Supreme Court—who interpret the Constitution according to its original intent. A justice who does not respect the original intent of the Constitution and who feels free to legislate from the bench is a loose cannon on a rolling deck. You never know when such a judge might decide to give Sharia law precedence over the Constitution.

As Christians, we should welcome and befriend our Muslim neighbors and coworkers. In the Old Testament, God told Israel, "When a foreigner resides among you in your land, do not mistreat them. The foreigner residing among you must be treated as your native-born. Love them as yourself, for you were foreigners in Egypt. I am the LORD your God."[25] And Jesus said, "For I was hungry and you gave me something to eat, I was thirsty and you gave me something to drink, I was a stranger and you invited me in."[26]

Though Muslims in the United States have the same rights and freedoms as other Americans, and though we are commanded to welcome the strangers among us, this doesn't mean we must support the mass migration of Muslim refugees to the West from war-torn nations like Syria, Iraq, Yemen, and Libya. Genuine compassion would require Western nations to help create "zones of protection" for refugees in those troubled countries. Our goal should be to repatriate the refugees once the humanitarian crisis is over. When refugees are uprooted from their own culture and resettled in the West, we invariably discover that a number of these "refugees" aren't refugees at all but Islamist terrorists. We have seen the result in a series of violent Islamist attacks in London, Paris, Nice, Brussels, Munich, and other Western cities.

We need to apply the First Amendment fairly to all religions, interpret the Constitution strictly according to its original intent, and avoid importing large numbers of people who do not respect our Western values, rights, and freedoms. Let's show Christian compassion to families fleeing from civil wars and terrorism—but let's also safeguard the security and freedom of our own families here in the West.

Public school or taxpayer-funded madrassa?

There is no separation of mosque and state in the Islamist mind-set. That is why, again and again, we see Islamists living in Western countries carrying signs that read, "Freedom go to hell!" And that is why, down through the centuries, Islam has been spread by the sword and by subterfuge.

One of the most devious forms of subterfuge is the effort to control the minds and hearts of our schoolchildren. Tragically, agencies of our own government, from the federal level to the local level, have aided and abetted this attack on our children. A prime example is a program called Access Islam, introduced years ago in the public schools by the United States Department of Education. Access Islam provides lesson plans with a video series produced by PBS affiliate Thirteen/WNET in New York. The lesson plans, designed for grades five through twelve, teach the Five Pillars of Islam, have students study verses from the Koran and recite the meaning of those verses, and focus on the Muslim five-times-daily prayer ritual.

In 2017, the PolitiFact.com website (founded by the *Tampa Bay Times* and now operated by the Poynter Institute) analyzed the Access Islam materials after conservative groups claimed that Access Islam was indoctrinating schoolchildren. PolitiFact concluded that there was no indoctrination taking place and quoted Diane Moore, director of Harvard Divinity School's Religious Literacy Project: "When any religious tradition is only represented in its positive light, it can feel like indoctrination to those who don't believe the tradition has merit or has equal credibility to one's own faith."[27]

But is Access Islam factually accurate if it represents Islam "only . . . in its positive light"? Does Access Islam discuss the violent early history of Islam; the First and Second Jihads; the fact that Islam has traditionally been propagated by the sword; the fact that women are oppressed and homosexuals are executed under Sharia law; the fact that a literal fundamentalist interpretation of passages in the Koran made the 9/11 attacks possible; and the fact that stealth jihad, cultural jihad, and dawa are the primary means by which the Third Jihad is being waged today?

No. If Access Islam presented the Islamic religion in anything but a "positive light," Muslims would be offended. But distorting the truth about Islam and presenting cherry-picked facts that cast Islam only in a positive light is at best propaganda. If it is impossible to *accurately* represent Islam to schoolchildren; if we must present a distorted and partial picture of the truth to avoid causing offense to Muslims, then perhaps we should ask ourselves: Does a sugarcoated, misleading representation of Islam belong in our public schools?

In truth, there is more to the Access Islam materials than simply presenting Islam in a "positive light." For example, PolitiFact ignored a video segment entitled "Hajj, Part I," which introduces an American-born man who converted from Christianity to Islam. Here's a partial transcript of that segment:

ANISA MEHDI: Abdul Alim Mubarak chose Islam when he was twenty-one. . . . He was born Ronald Carl Rowe in Richmond,

Virginia. He took his Muslim name when he turned forty. His conversion to Islam came amid the political and social upheaval of the '60s civil rights movement and Malcolm X's pilgrimage to Mecca. By 1973, this American-born Christian had found a new path.

MR. MUBARAK: I said, "Hah, this is it! This is what I've been searching for. This is what I want."

MEHDI: What about it made it "it"?

MR. MUBARAK: The respect for the intellect, respect for the true worship of God with no intercessors, with no intermediaries, the simplicity of it all.

AUDREY ROWE: Oh, that sounds promising, yes?

MEHDI: Audrey Rowe, Mubarak's wife of 17 years, is a devout Christian. Their daughter, Selana, studies both faiths. Mubarak is taking three weeks off from his job as an editor for CNN. He's finding that his colleagues are learning something about Islam by watching him practice his faith.

MUBARAK: I'm level-headed. I'm not a fanatic. I worship the same God that many of them do.[28]

The message of this segment is clear: "Students, this man traded his Christian faith for the Muslim religion—and you can too! And see, he even gets along well with a Christian wife and a daughter who doesn't know what to believe. Isn't this a beautiful utopian dream? And did you hear what this Muslim man said, students? Islam is better than Christianity because Islam shows respect for the intellect and respect for the true worship of God with no intercessors or intermediaries." How is this not indoctrination?

Who are we trying to kid? How can the perpetrators of this propaganda claim with a straight face that they are not trying to indoctrinate our schoolchildren? I wouldn't be at all surprised to learn one day that Access Islam has been a factor in turning many young people to Islam. At the very least, this saccharine-sweet image of Islam helps to allay the wariness that American schoolkids ought to have toward Islamist propaganda efforts.

In a rational world—a world not run by the secular left—schools would teach our young people how to use critical thinking skills with regard to Islam. Instead, with Access Islam, they're teaching only an uncritical sweetness-and-light version of Islam.

Even more troubling, individual schools often take the Access Islam curriculum even further toward indoctrination than was intended. Radio and television commentator Todd Starnes reported on a case at La Plata High School, a public school in Charles County, Maryland. There, students are required to recite the Shahada (which means "to testify").[29] The Shahada is an Islamic creed that states, "I testify that there is no God but Allah, and I testify that Muhammad is the Messenger of Allah."[30] Christian students should understand that the Shahada is, for them, a blasphemous statement that disparages their own faith. In some Muslim circles, reciting the Shahada before witnesses constitutes conversion to Islam.

In October 2014, John and Melissa Wood were dismayed when their daughter showed them some assignments from her eleventh-grade world history class. One of the printed handouts, titled "Islam Today," contained several statements including "Islam, at heart, is a peaceful religion" and "Most Muslims' faith is stronger than the average Christian['s]."[31] The first statement is Islamist propaganda, and the second is pro-Islamic, anti-Christian indoctrination. Both statements are unsubstantiated.

The school also taught that Allah in Islam is identical to the God of Judaism and Christianity. Anyone who has ever made an honest, side-by-side comparison of the attributes of Allah versus the attributes of God knows this isn't so. As Todd Starnes concludes, "It sounds as if somebody turned La Plata High School into a taxpayer-funded Madrassa."[32]

It gets worse. When John Wood—a Marine veteran who lost close friends in combat during Operation Desert Storm—called the school to voice his concerns about his daughter's classroom assignments and asked that his daughter be exempted from the lessons and allowed to do an alternative assignment, the vice principal told him the class work was a nonnegotiable requirement and his daughter would either complete the assignments or receive a failing grade. It didn't matter that the assignments violated the family's Christian beliefs.

A later phone call from the school's resource officer (a police officer assigned to the school) informed John Wood that a no-trespass order had been issued against him and he would not be allowed on school property for any reason. Wood does not understand why he was barred from coming on campus—he contends he never did or said anything inappropriate, nor did he give school officials any reason to think he posed a physical threat. The only "threat" he made was that he was considering his legal remedies and might take his case to the media.

Did La Plata High School also teach about Christianity in its eleventh-grade world history class? Yes, in fact, it did—but in a slanted, prejudicial way. According to a brief filed on behalf of the Wood family by the Thomas More Law Center, "During its brief instruction on Christianity, defendants failed to cover any portion of the Bible or other non-Islamic religious texts, such as the Ten Commandments. Instead, the class included disparaging remarks about Christianity and the Pope."[33]

Starnes concludes by asking why secular left organizations such as the Freedom from Religion Foundation and the American Civil Liberties Union haven't "weighed in" to oppose religious indoctrination in a public high school. "Their silence is peculiar," he writes. "I suspect their reaction would have been a bit different had La Plata High School been baptizing children and forcing them to memorize John 3:16."[34]

Undoubtedly so. The secular left is fanatically obsessed with separation of church and state but seems strangely sympathetic to the merging of mosque and state. In the next chapter, we will get to the root of this bizarre inconsistency in liberal-progressive thinking.

10

THE SECULAR-ISLAMIST ALLIANCE

ON OCTOBER 23, 1995, Congress passed the Jerusalem Embassy Act, defining the policy of the United States toward the city of Jerusalem—that it "should remain an undivided city in which the rights of every ethnic and religious group are protected; . . . be recognized as the capital of the State of Israel; and [that] the United States Embassy in Israel should be established in Jerusalem no later than May 31, 1999."[1] The bill was adopted by the Senate on a vote of ninety-three to five and by the House on a vote of 374 to thirty-seven. Passed by veto-proof margins, it became law, without President Clinton's signature, on November 8, 1995.

Despite passage of the law in 1995, the American embassy did not open in Jerusalem until 2018. Why?

There was a provision in the law that allowed the president

to sign a series of six-month waivers on implementation. So, beginning with Bill Clinton, American presidents signed waiver after waiver, every six months, administration after administration, delaying the transfer of the embassy for nearly two decades.

On December 6, 2017, President Donald Trump formally recognized Jerusalem as the capital of Israel and ordered preparations for the relocation of the embassy as required by law. Five months later, on May 14, 2018—the seventieth anniversary of the founding of the state of Israel—the American embassy opened in Jerusalem.

If you were watching TV news or reading a newspaper that day, it's unlikely you heard any of the history I just recounted. The Jerusalem embassy story was largely reported as if President Trump, without congressional authorization, acted thoughtlessly and irrationally. This statement from National Public Radio was typical of media coverage: "Trump announced last December that he would break with the consensus of America's allies and decades of tradition by recognizing Jerusalem as the official capital and moving the embassy there from Tel Aviv."[2]

The point is this: When you read the mainstream media's stories about events in the Middle East, you must dig deeper than the misleading headlines, and you must read with great discernment.

Where has all the money gone?

On the same day the embassy in Jerusalem opened for business, the terror group Hamas staged a deadly protest along the fence dividing Israel and Gaza. Though Israeli aircraft had dropped leaflets warning the Palestinians to keep their distance, more than forty thousand Hamas-led protesters assembled at a dozen places along the border fence. Hamas even sent children to the fence. Protesters threw rocks and firebombs or rolled burning tires at the fence, hoping to break through the razor-wire. Fifty-nine protesters died and 2,400 were injured when Israeli forces opened fire to prevent the Palestinians from breaching the barrier. Among the dead: two children, ages twelve and fourteen.

Hamas had organized weekly protests every Friday since March 30, leading up to the anniversary of Israel's founding. The Palestinians refer to Israel's founding as *Nakba* ("The Catastrophe"), when more than seven hundred thousand Palestinian Arab Muslims fled Israel and became refugees in neighboring Jordan, Lebanon, and Egypt. But not all fled. Some Palestinian Arabs remained in Israel, and the group now amounts to more than one-fifth of Israel's population.

The Palestinians have suffered greatly—but mostly at the hands of their own corrupt leaders. As US Ambassador to the UN Nikki Haley told the UN Security Council in April 2018, "Anyone who truly cares about children in Gaza should insist that Hamas immediately stop using children as cannon fodder in its conflict with Israel. . . . It's difficult to think of a more cowardly act—even for a terrorist—than hiding behind innocent civilians."[3]

Palestinian leaders have a long history of abusing their own people. A 2004 report on *60 Minutes* revealed that Yasser Arafat, chairman of the Palestine Liberation Organization, raked in hundreds of millions (and perhaps multiple billions) of dollars, and little if any of that money went to improve the lives of the Palestinian people. Arafat also had investments in a Coca-Cola bottling plant in the West Bank, a cell phone company in Tunisia, and capital funds in the Caymans.

Under the terms of the 1993 Oslo Accords, Arafat received tax revenue collected by the Israeli government—money that was supposed to help the Palestinian people. That revenue became Arafat's personal slush fund, deposited at Bank Leumi in Tel Aviv before being transferred to a secret account at Lombard Odier Bank in Switzerland, accessible only by Arafat.

According to the *60 Minutes* report, Arafat doled out money "like a Chicago ward boss," maintaining his power by paying his security forces in cash. American officials estimated his personal net worth at between $1 billion and $3 billion. Though Arafat lived a spartan lifestyle in a walled compound in the West Bank, his wife lived lavishly in Paris on an allowance of $100,000 a month.

Arafat's relatives and associates controlled the Palestinian economy with a system of monopolies. One Arafat crony controlled the flour market, another controlled cement, and so on. An Arafat associate also headed General Petroleum Corporation, the only gasoline supplier in Palestine. The corporation, said *60 Minutes*, "charged exorbitant prices, and Arafat got a hefty kickback." The company purchased gasoline from an Israeli company, diluted it with cheap kerosene, and sold it to the Palestinians at inflated prices. Over time, the gasoline-kerosene mix damaged the engines of the Palestinians' cars. Despite his wealth, Arafat continually claimed the Palestinian government was bankrupt in order to wring more cash out of the international community.[4]

In 2005, after Arafat's death, the World Bank announced that the international community would invest $750 million in Gaza as "an expression of hope for the future." The money from eight industrialized nations would create jobs, build roads and water projects, and construct houses. The eight nations also pledged up to $9 billion of private investment in Gaza over three years.[5]

How did that project work out? In 2018, the World Bank reported, "Gaza has seen conditions steadily deteriorate over the last two decades, leading to collapsing of the economy and basic social services." Today, the economy of Gaza is stagnant, half the work force is unemployed, water and electricity are rationed, and the Palestinians are in utter despair.[6] Yet billions of dollars continue to pour into that tiny strip of land.

If the Palestinians and their leaders were not so bent on pushing Israel into the sea, they could have used all those billions to turn Gaza into a fabulous resort, a Mediterranean destination for the world to enjoy. The Palestinians could have full employment and enormous prosperity. Instead, they have chosen squalor for themselves and hopelessness for their children while blaming Israel for their woes.

According to a 2016 article in the *Wall Street Journal*, the Palestinians receive far more money from Europe and America (in so-called development assistance) than any other impoverished group.

> The disproportionate share of development assistance the Palestinians receive . . . comes at the expense of needy populations elsewhere. According to a report last year by Global Humanitarian

Assistance, in 2013 the Palestinians received $793 million in international aid, second only to Syria. This amounts to $176 for each Palestinian, by far the highest per capita assistance in the world. Syria . . . received only $106 per capita.

A closer look at the remaining eight countries in the top ten—Sudan, South Sudan, Jordan, Lebanon, Somalia, Ethiopia, Afghanistan and the Democratic Republic of Congo—is even more alarming. CIA Factbook data show that these countries have a combined population of 284 million and an average per capita GDP of $2,376. Yet they received an average of $15.30 per capita in development assistance in 2013. The Palestinians, by comparison, with a population of 4.5 million, have a per capita GDP of $4,900.

In other words, though the Palestinians are more than twice as wealthy on average than these eight countries, they receive *more than 11 times as much foreign aid per person.*[7]

Millions of dollars continue to be funneled to the Palestinians, yet the money vanishes into a black hole, and the Palestinians' lives never improve. Where does the money go? Palestinian leaders spend it on guns, ammunition, and rockets. They pay terrorists to kill Jews on buses or in the streets. They invest in jihad and reap dividends of poverty and death.

Leftist bias and the Israeli-Palestinian narrative

The coverage of the Israeli-Palestinian conflict in the left-leaning news media always follows a predetermined narrative. American journalist Hunter Stuart describes that narrative in an opinion piece for the *Jerusalem Post*:

Being liberal in America comes with a pantheon of beliefs: You support pluralism, tolerance and diversity. You support gay rights, access to abortion and gun control.

The belief that Israel is unjustly bullying the Palestinians is an inextricable part of this pantheon. Most progressives in the US view Israel as an aggressor, oppressing the poor noble Arabs who are being so brutally denied their freedom.[8]

Hunter Stuart and his wife lived in Jerusalem for a year and half, beginning in mid-2015. He believed that if Israel would stop occupying the West Bank and tear down the fence between Israel and Gaza, Palestinian unrest would end.

In October 2015, a wave of Palestinian attacks swept Jerusalem. Young Palestinian Muslims went on a stabbing rampage or ran people down with cars. This wave of violence, known as the Stabbing Intifada, began to change Stuart's thinking.

Once, while researching a news story, he visited an impoverished Palestinian neighborhood in East Jerusalem. A Palestinian boy about thirteen years old pointed at him and shouted in Arabic, *"Yehud! Yehud!* (Jew! Jew!)" Instantly, other Palestinians surrounded him, shouting, *"Yehud! Yehud!"* The look in their eyes filled Stuart with panic. He shouted, *"Ana mish yehud!* (I'm not Jewish!)" When he told them he was an American journalist who loved the Palestinian people, they stopped berating him. Sometime later, he told a Palestinian friend about his experience. His friend replied, "If you were Jewish, they probably would have killed you."

Soon afterward, Stuart learned of the murder of Richard Lakin, an American who loved the Palestinian people, attended peace rallies, and taught Palestinian children in a Jerusalem school. The killers were paid twenty thousand shekels to storm a Jerusalem bus and shoot or stab the passengers. Lakin died and ten others on the bus were wounded. The killers were glorified as heroes on posters in East Jerusalem—for killing a man who only wanted to help the Palestinians.

Stuart became acutely aware of the anti-Israeli, pro-Palestinian bias pervading the news industry. Editors wanted stories that fit one narrative: Israel is to blame for Palestinian violence. He noticed the same bias among European leaders and humanitarian organizations. Amnesty International, for example, regularly condemns Israel for its "shoot to kill" policy toward terrorists but never condemns England, France, Egypt, or the United States for following identical policies.

Why do liberals apply a double standard to Israel compared to all the other nations in the world? Hunter Stuart offers an explanation: "The Israeli-Palestinian conflict appeals to the appetites of progressive people in Europe, the US, and elsewhere. They see it as a white, first-world people beating on a poor, third-world one. It's easier for them to become outraged watching two radically different civilizations collide than it is watching Alawite Muslims kill Sunni Muslims in Syria, for example."[9]

Stuart concludes that it ultimately comes down to "the liberal desire to support the underdog." There's a name for this phenomenon: *underdogma.*

I wrote about underdogma in my previous book, *The Hidden Enemy*, but it's worth revisiting. The term was coined by columnist Michael Prell in his book titled *Underdogma*. Prell observes that liberals divide people into two opposing camps—strong versus weak, powerful versus powerless, overdog versus underdog. Underdogma is the "reflexive opposition to the more powerful overdog, and automatic support for the less powerful underdog. . . . Underdogma is about power imbalances. And there are few places on Earth where the balance of power is drawn in starker contrast than . . . the Israeli-Palestinian conflict."[10]

Islamism—fundamentalist political Islam—is deeply entrenched in the Palestinian culture. Islamists oppress women and execute homosexuals. They despise Jews with an intensity scarcely matched by the Nazis. They are rigidly opposed to all the values liberals and progressives hold dear. Yet liberals maintain an irrational solidarity with the Palestinian Islamists, a solidarity based solely (it would seem) on underdogma.

Instead of asking, "Who is the underdog in this conflict?" we should ask who is right, who is wrong, who acts justly, and who behaves unjustly. Yes, the Palestinians are the weak, impoverished underdogs—but that doesn't make the murder of Jews and the annihilation of Israel a just cause. Truth—not underdogma—is the only legitimate basis for deciding who's right and who's wrong.

The jizya tax and the welfare state

The secular left has made a devil's bargain with political Islam. What do the Islamists and the secular left have in common? Just this: Both want to overthrow traditional Western culture and Judeo-Christian values. As a result, the Islamists are using our liberal institutions against us—the welfare state, liberal notions of multiculturalism, and liberal rules of political correctness.

In 2018, a TV reporter for Fox 9 Minneapolis–St. Paul

received a tip that Somali travelers were routinely departing from the Minneapolis airport carrying suitcases stuffed with one million dollars in cash. These cash shipments left once or twice a week—more than one-hundred million dollars in 2017 alone.

There's nothing illegal about traveling with that much cash—but where did that money come from? And where was it going?

The source of the money, it turned out, was a massive welfare fraud scheme, and much of it went to a region in Somalia controlled by the al-Shabaab terrorist group.

The state of Minnesota is known for its liberal welfare benefits and loose requirements. As a result, millions of taxpayer dollars had flown overseas to fund jihad. The scheme involved government-funded daycare centers that would sign up low-income Somali families who qualified for assistance, but the families would rarely show up. Still, the center billed the state, and the cash ended up in suitcases at the airport.

One daycare operator, Fozia Ali, was believed to have bilked the state of Minnesota out of more than a million dollars for childcare services she never rendered. She used some of the money to travel overseas, and she was able to bill for non-existent services while she was in Dubai and Kenya, using a government-supplied app on her phone. She is currently serving time in federal prison.

Fox 9 reporter Jeff Baillon concluded, "Sources in the Somali community told [us] it is an open secret that starting a daycare center is a license to make money. . . . Government insiders believe this scam is costing the state at least a hundred million dollars a year, half of all child-care subsidies. . . . Fraudsters in other states are now using the Minnesota playbook to rip off millions of public dollars meant to help kids."[11]

European countries and Canada also have generous welfare programs that are magnets for Islamists. Take Belgium, for example. As *Investor's Business Daily* reports:

> Belgium's government has been extremely generous toward its Muslim population. Most of its welfare goes to Muslims, and it even subsidizes their mosques and imams.
>
> Many of these young Muslim men who supposedly can't find gainful employment don't want to work. Why would they, when welfare checks are normally 70% to 80% of their income? . . .
>
> By not holding regular jobs, they have time to make "hijrah" to Syria, where they can train for jihad and return with other "skills" like manufacturing nail bombs in safe houses unmolested by authorities (who agree not to make raids at night out of respect for Muslim neighborhoods).[12]

A story in the *Toronto Sun* told of hundreds of Muslim men in Toronto who had polygamous marriages and collected welfare benefits for each wife. The generous provisions of the Ontario Family Law Act allow Muslim men with multiple wives to live off Canadian taxpayers, even though polygamy is illegal in Canada. As long as the polygamous union was legal in the country where the weddings took place, the welfare state would pay. Technically, a welfare recipient can claim only one spouse—but the other wives in the harem can collect by making independent applications. A wife with one child receives about $1,500 per month.

Attorney Syed Mumtaz Ali, then president of the Canadian Society of Muslims, encouraged Muslims to take advantage of the Canadian taxpayers. "This is a law and there's nothing wrong with it," he said. "Canada is a very liberal-minded country."[13]

The British welfare system is also very generous—and British Islamists are proud to take advantage of it. When five Muslim extremists were convicted of harassment for protesting dead British soldiers coming home from the Iraq War, the extremists boasted that they were "on benefits" (receiving British welfare). They didn't care that the judge had ordered them to pay £500 in costs. "The taxpayer paid for this court case," one defendant sneered. "The taxpayer will pay for the fines, too, out of benefits."[14]

It's no accident that Islamists take advantage of the liberal welfare state. It's a deliberate strategy. British Muslim cleric and activist Anjem Choudary was convicted of recruiting support for ISIS and is now serving time. He has four children and at one time collected £25,000 per year (about $39,000 US) in British welfare benefits.

In 2013, Choudary was secretly recorded encouraging his followers to collect what he called the "Jihadi Seekers Allowance" (from Jobseeker's Allowance, the British term for unemployment benefits) rather than work full time. He described the welfare system payouts as a jizya, the tax of submission that the Koran demands non-Muslims pay to Muslims as a sign of submission. Reflecting the Islamist attitude toward British taxpayers, Choudary said, "The normal situation . . . really is to take money from the *kuffar* [an insulting term for non-Muslims], isn't it? So this is normal situation. They give us the money—you work, give us the money. Allah Akbar, we take the money."[15]

Multiculturalism or melting pot?

Leftist policies serve the jihadist cause in many ways. One example is the liberal "open borders" agenda—the effort to maintain lax immigration policies, sanctuary cities and sanctuary states, and the effort to thwart security measures at our nation's borders. Some leftists advocate wide-open borders—no restrictions whatsoever. Leftists promote these notions not with logical arguments, but with simple-minded slogans like, "Build bridges, not walls!"

During the May Day 2018 parade in Minneapolis, far-left Congressman Keith Ellison was on the street greeting constituents, wearing a black shirt emblazoned with a slogan in Spanish: *"Yo no creo en fronteras."* English translation: "I don't believe in borders." Ellison, the nation's first Muslim congressman, was elected deputy chairman of the Democratic National Committee in 2017, even though his radical views are far to the left of his party's mainstream. A January 2018 Harvard-Harris Poll found that only 32 percent of Democrats agree with Ellison that America's borders should be wide open.[16]

Borders matter. Victor Davis Hanson, a Hoover Institution fellow, writes, "Borders are to distinct countries what fences are to neighbors: means of demarcating that something on one side is different from what lies on the other side."[17]

The cities of San Diego and Tijuana sit virtually side by side on the Pacific coast, separated by the United States–Mexico border. These two cities have identical weather, beaches, and natural resources. They should be identical twin cities, but they are worlds apart. San Diego is a city of colleges and universities, museums, professional sports teams, golf courses and country clubs, TV and radio stations, conventions, and financial institutions. According to the FBI, San Diego is the safest major city in America, with an annual murder rate of 3.6 murders per one hundred thousand people. By contrast, Tijuana is the fifth most dangerous city in the world, with a rate of 100.77 murders per one hundred thousand people.[18] The city is steeped in poverty, crime, drug abuse, and political corruption.

All that separates San Diego and Tijuana is a border fence—but what a difference the fence makes. On one side of the border is the American Constitution, American values, American law, and the American social structure. These same values, laws, and social structure are attainable for the people on the other side of the border fence. They would have much better lives if the government of Mexico would study and emulate the example set by the United States.

Another example: Have you ever seen a satellite photo of the Korean Peninsula at night? It's a stunning illustration of why borders matter. A distinct line of demarcation divides North and South Korea. Nighttime South Korea is ablaze in electric lights, symbolizing the robust economic activity that accompanies freedom. North Korea is as dark as a coal sack—a vivid demonstration of the poverty and hopelessness of life under a Communist dictatorship.[19]

If you talk about illegal immigration as a problem in America, odds are someone will brand you a "racist" or a "xenophobe." As an Egyptian-born *legal* immigrant and naturalized American citizen, I thank God for the path of legal immigration I've been able to follow. But I tremble to think of the dangers posed to America if the left ever gets its way and flings open the borders of this nation. Not only does lax border security invite criminal gangs and cartels into America while driving down wages for Americans and legal immigrants, but it also threatens America's safety and security.

We often assume that illegal immigrants come only from Mexico, Central America, and other Latin American countries. In recent years, however, federal agents have detained increasing numbers of so-called *special interest aliens*, who sneak into the country from hotbeds of militant Islam: Iran, Pakistan, and Syria. In 2015 alone, federal agents detained 3,977 people from nations classified by the US government as "countries of interest" or "state sponsors of terrorism." According to the Department of Homeland Security, from 2006 through 2015, 67,180 people from fourteen nations were apprehended who had illegally crossed the southern border.[20]

So far, there has not been an attack by a Muslim terrorist who illegally crossed the US–Mexico border. But such an attack could happen at any time. Moreover, jihadists want to enter the US and other Western countries for many reasons—to raise money for Islamist causes, to train and recruit jihadists, or to preach Islamist doctrines and radicalize moderate Muslims. As Rick Perry, then governor of Texas, told President Obama in 2010, "An unsecured border is a threat to our national security and to the safety and security of all our citizens."[21]

Among the radical Islamists who have been detained at America's southern border in recent years were members of the East African terror group al-Shabaab (which carried out a deadly 2013 shopping mall attack in Nairobi, Kenya), members of the radical Kurdish Workers' Party, and two Pakistanis with terrorist ties, Muhammad Azeem and Mukhtar Ahmad.[22]

Another leftist notion that aids the jihadist cause is multi-culturalism. In America, we have always celebrated cultural diversity. I came from an Arab Christian culture in Egypt. Over the years, I have traveled around the world, and I have always enjoyed discovering the foods, traditions, ideas, and history of other cultures. When I came to the United States, I discovered that every culture in the world has found a welcoming home here in America. What has traditionally made America unique is a concept we are in danger of losing—the idea of America, the Great Melting Pot.

The melting pot metaphor was conceived by the Jewish playwright Israel Zangwill, whose parents emigrated to London from Russia and Poland. In his plays, Zangwill championed the cause of oppressed people, including women and his own Jewish community. He popularized a utopian vision of American equality and diversity in his 1908 play, *The Melting Pot*. It was a reworking of Shakespeare's *Romeo and Juliet*, set in New York City, about two people who fall in love and overcome the cultural attitudes of their families. Zangwill expressed his view in these lines of dialogue: "A fig for your feuds and vendettas. Germans and Frenchmen, Irishmen and Englishmen, Jews and Russians—into the Crucible with you all: God is making the American."[23]

People have come together on the North American continent from all over the world—Native Americans, Europeans,

Africans, Asians—and in this crucible is forged an American ideal and identity. As we respect each other, learn from each other, and appreciate each other's traditions, we grow stronger together.

Clearly the American people and government have not always lived up to the American ideal. The history of this nation is stained with the sweat and blood of slaves. Immigrants from many lands have been mistreated and exploited on American soil. Racism and segregation are an undeniable part of our nation's tragic legacy. But it is the American ideal of the melting pot that has enabled us to overcome these dark legacies. The melting pot ideal is founded on that uniquely American declaration on July 4, 1776, that we are all created equal, that we are endowed by our Creator with certain unalienable rights.

Today, the political left rejects the melting pot idea in favor of an opposing concept: *multiculturalism*. Multiculturalism superficially resembles the melting pot, but where the melting pot enables people from different backgrounds and traditions to assimilate and unify around a common identity as Americans, multiculturalism encourages fragmentation and division. Multiculturalism leads to "identity politics," in which Americans separate into competing tribal groups according to their so-called identity—their ethnicity, language, culture, national origin, sexual orientation, or whatever other line of demarcation they can find.

The melting pot celebrated unity in the midst of diversity. Multiculturalism and identity politics pit one culture against another, one identity against another, one ethnicity against another, one generation against another. Multiculturalism undercuts our American unity. Identity politics leads to feuds and vendettas.

Multiculturalism and identity politics promote the idea that you are who you are because of your race, ethnicity, or gender orientation. This leads to the notion that some groups are *privileged* while others are *victims*. Again, we can't deny a legacy of past discrimination and injustice—and yes, racism still exists in our society today. But no nation on earth has fought harder to eliminate injustice and provide equal opportunity for all than the United States of America. Tragically, many who think they are victims of an unjust society have never been taught how to access the opportunities that are all around them.

This takes us back to underdogma, in which we look at people not as individuals, but as members of an "underdog" or "victim" group. If you're doing well and making a good living, it's not because you worked hard and made good choices—it's because you have a "racial privilege." If you're struggling economically, it's because you're a victim of an oppressive Western culture. As economist Thomas Sowell wryly observes, "What 'multiculturalism' boils down to is that you can praise any culture in the world except Western culture—and you cannot blame any culture in the world except Western culture."[24]

Multiculturalism and identity politics lead to a culture of grievance. Taken to its logical extreme, a culture of grievance produces a mind-set like we see among the Palestinians toward the nation of Israel. It causes hatred, division, and cycles of attack and revenge. In grievance politics, it's always someone else's fault. We see what the culture of grievance has produced in the Gaza Strip—death, poverty, and hopelessness. We now see this same pattern of grievance in America, in groups like Black Lives Matter and Antifa and others, wherever the poisonous doctrine of multiculturalism takes hold. We need a return to the melting pot vision of America, which seeks to heal divisions, bring marginalized people into the mainstream, and affirm our differences while strengthening our unity.

All too often, left-leaning educators have taught young people that America is a racist country, built on slavery and segregation, the source of most of the evils in the world. As a result, many of our young people today are growing up without hearing that it's the genius of the American founding documents—the notion that "all men are created equal, that they are endowed by their Creator with certain unalienable Rights"—that drove America to fight a bloody civil war to do away with slavery. Those words also ignited the grand dream of Dr. Martin Luther King Jr. and led to the end of segregation.

Slavery is alive and well in many parts of the world, especially the Muslim world. But America outlawed slavery long ago. Yes, there have been many shameful episodes in American history, as there are in the history of every nation on the planet. But the legacy of America is how the culturally diverse American people came together and sought to do away with these oppressive institutions. That's why we should rid ourselves of the myth of multiculturalism and return to the unifying principle of the melting pot.

The moral insanity of political correctness

On August 3, 2018, authorities raided a compound of ramshackle buildings in a remote desert of New Mexico. There they arrested an American Muslim, Siraj Ibn Wahhaj, and four other adults on charges of child abuse. Wahhaj was also wanted for kidnapping his three-year-old son from the boy's mother's home in Georgia.

Eleven children, ages one through fifteen, were found alive but seriously malnourished at the compound. They had been living for months in filthy rags, without running water or electricity. The badly decomposed body of a twelfth child was found in a grave at the compound. The dead child, investigators found, was the three-year-old boy Wahhaj had kidnapped. According to the Georgia arrest warrant, Wahhaj told the child's mother he planned to exorcise the child of a devil. (The boy was prone to seizures, which were being controlled with medication.)

Wahhaj is the son of a notorious Brooklyn imam who may have been a coconspirator in the 1993 World Trade Center bombing, according to court documents. Though there was no food at the compound, investigators said Wahhaj had an arsenal of firearms and ammunition. According to documents filed by the prosecutors, Wahhaj was training the children to carry out mass shootings at schools.[25]

I don't find it surprising that these radical Islamists were abusing children and training them to commit murder in the name of Allah. But what the American legal system did in response to this arrest is a shock to the conscience and to logic.

The court-appointed defense attorney argued that the defendants should be released on grounds of—are you ready for this?—the First and Second Amendments.

"If these were white people of a Christian faith who owned guns," the lawyer said, "that's not a big deal because there's a

Second Amendment right to own firearms in this country. . . . We have freedom of religion in this country. But they look different and they worship differently from the rest of us. When black Muslims do it there seems to be something nefarious, something evil."[26]

Is that true? Could a white, supposedly Christian group starve and neglect children, kidnap a child who is later found dead and secretly buried more than two thousand miles from home, and train other children to use guns, allegedly to commit mass murder—and simply be turned loose on the public? Not in any sane courtroom. The defense argument was foolish, outrageous nonsense—but the judge bought it and set bail at a mere $20,000.

But wait—it gets worse: The dollar figure was merely symbolic. The judge allowed the defendants to walk out of court on a signature bond—which means *they didn't have to post any cash*. The judge required them to wear GPS ankle monitors, and they were technically under house arrest—but they had no house to go to. Their "house" was a filthy shack in the New Mexico desert, and they were forbidden to go back there. The ruling was nonsensical at every level.[27]

I ask you: Did Siraj Ibn Wahhaj and the other adults in that compound pose a danger to the community? Did they pose a risk of fleeing from justice? What do you think? More to the point, what was *the judge* thinking?

I can't read the judge's mind, but I can't help but think she was bending over backward to avoid being called an Islamophobe. Perhaps she chose to violate all logic and common sense in a contorted effort to remain politically correct.

When I first heard the term *politically correct*, I thought it was a joke. In a free society like America, there is no single "politically correct" point of view. Everyone is free to form his or her own opinions. In a PC world, there would be only one opinion—the "correct" one—and we would all have to agree with it, or else. So when I first heard the term, I didn't think anyone would seriously suggest such a notion.

I was wrong. The term has been used in academic circles since the 1970s as a way of imposing leftist orthodoxy. The notion that we must all think "correctly" about certain issues has become entrenched in Western culture, especially in our universities, political institutions, and newsrooms. And because political correctness requires us to view Muslims as underdogs to whom we must defer, the PC mind-set has done great harm. It has even killed innocent people.

Case in point: On November 5, 2009, US Army major Nidal Malik Hasan, an American-born Muslim, went on a murderous rampage at Fort Hood, Texas. He fatally shot thirteen people and wounded more than thirty before being shot by base police. His wounds left him paralyzed, and he was convicted of murder and sentenced to death. Prior to the attack, the shooter had made repeated contact with al-Qaeda leader Anwar al-Awlaki, and he shouted "Allahu Akbar!" as he carried out the attack. Any rational person would call this man a terrorist.

But political correctness negates reason. The US Army concluded that the attack was not terrorism—it was "workplace violence." Evidently, the Army feared that branding these murders an act of terrorism might be seen as a condemnation of Islam itself—and that would be politically incorrect.

After the shootings, the Army's chief of staff, General George Casey, made the rounds of the TV talk shows, including CNN's *State of the Union*. There he made a statement that was a masterpiece of political correctness: "Our diversity, not only in our Army, but in our country, is a strength. And as horrific as this tragedy was, if our diversity becomes a casualty, I think that's worse."[28]

In other words, in a PC world, diversity outweighs the thirteen lives lost in the Fort Hood massacre. Maintaining a multicultural Army is more important than those thirteen dead soldiers.

We later learned that Hasan's fellow soldiers had repeatedly complained about his violent and radical views. The FBI had monitored his email exchanges with Anwar al-Awlaki, who was later killed in a US drone strike in Afghanistan. Despite the warning signs, the Army promoted Hasan to the rank of major. Why? It appears it was because Hasan is a Muslim, an underdog, and failing to promote him might be perceived as politically incorrect. Had he been properly disciplined or discharged, those thirteen soldiers might not have died. And because the Army labeled Hasan's crime "workplace violence" instead of terrorism, the soldiers he killed and wounded at Fort Hood were denied the Purple Heart and additional benefits that accompany being wounded in action.[29]

Here's another horrifying example of PC insanity, this time from Great Britain: In 2014, a British government report disclosed that fourteen hundred girls in the town of Rotherham, South Yorkshire, had been sexually abused by gangs of Pakistani Muslim men. The abuse began in 1997 and continued for years.

The girls were often gang-raped, then driven to other towns and raped again. Some were as young as eleven. Girls who were reluctant to cooperate would be splashed with gasoline, then an assailant would flick a match and threaten to burn them alive.

And here's the most shocking fact of all: *The authorities knew it was happening.* Police knew. Social workers knew. But no one did anything to stop it.

One girl told how she was raped every week from age thirteen to fifteen. She had gone to the police three months after the weekly rapes began, and she gave the police her DNA-stained clothing as evidence. The police "lost" the clothing and told her the case would probably not go to court. Again and again, victims and parents reported crimes to police—and the police refused to act.

British social worker Alexis Jay is an instructor at the University of Strathclyde and chair of the Independent Inquiry into Child Sexual Abuse.[30] Her investigative team released a 153-page report on the rapes in Rotherham. They interviewed police and social workers who knew about the crimes but did nothing. Their excuse: They feared being labeled as racists if they even questioned Muslim men about the crimes. They obeyed the rigid rules of political correctness.

Their fears were well-founded. When member of Parliament Ann Cryer exposed a similar rape scandal involving Pakistani men in Keighley, West Yorkshire, political opponents attacked her. She said that the "politically correct Left just saw it as racism."[31] Another member of Parliament, Simon Danczuk of Rochdale, exposed an abuse scandal only to be condemned by opponents who, he said, were "obsessing about multiculturalism."[32]

The evidence proves there's an unspoken, unwitting alliance between the left and the Islamists. The Islamists knowingly exploit the welfare state, liberal immigration policies, and liberal notions of multiculturalism and political correctness to carry out the destruction of Western civilization.

I pray that the leaders in our government, law enforcement, and the news media will come to their senses, that the scales will fall from their eyes. I pray that moral sanity would be restored before it's too late.

11

THE KEY TO SURVIVAL

IN JANUARY 1838, twenty-eight-year-old Abraham Lincoln delivered a speech before the Young Men's Lyceum of Springfield, Illinois. In his speech, Lincoln made a prediction about the future of America—and the biggest threat facing America.

> Shall we expect some transatlantic military giant to step the
> Ocean and crush us at a blow? Never! All the armies of Europe,
> Asia and Africa combined, with all the treasure of the earth
> (our own excepted) in their military chest; with a [Napoleon]
> Bonaparte for a commander, could not by force take a drink
> from the Ohio, or make a track on the Blue Ridge, in a trial of
> a thousand years.
>
> At what point then is the approach of danger to be expected?
> I answer, if it ever reach us, it must spring up amongst us. It
> cannot come from abroad. If destruction be our lot, we must

ourselves be its author and finisher. As a nation of freemen, we
must live through all time, or die by suicide.[1]

I believe young Mr. Lincoln's words with all my being. I
don't believe America will ever be destroyed solely by an attack
from a foreign nation or a foreign-based terror organization.
Terrorists may hijack our airplanes, knock down our buildings,
and even kill our countrymen with weapons of mass destruction. But terrorists do not have the power to destroy our nation.
If America dies, it will die because of the self-destructive choices
we make as a free people.

My fear is that the slow suicide of America has already begun.
We are losing our nation the same way the ancient Israelites lost
theirs in the days before the Babylonians destroyed Jerusalem
and led the people into captivity. We are losing America the
same way the ancient Romans lost their empire when it fell to
the barbarian hordes.

How did these other great civilizations commit suicide?
They died by becoming morally corrupt and spiritually indifferent. Will ours be the generation that destroys what the founding
fathers risked everything to build?

When the collapse of America comes, it will catch most
Americans by surprise. It will seem to happen suddenly, without
warning—but in fact the slow crumbling of America's moral
and spiritual foundation is already well under way.

In Ernest Hemingway's *The Sun Also Rises*, two characters
have a conversation about bankruptcy. Bill Gorton asks, "How
did you go bankrupt?" Mike Campbell replies, "Two ways.
Gradually and then suddenly."[2]

That is how most collapses occur—gradually and then suddenly. Before a person goes bankrupt, he or she makes thousands of bad decisions over a period of years. The consequences of those bad decisions slowly accumulate, gradually weighing the person down with debt. Finally, the debt reaches a critical mass, and the financial house of cards collapses. Nations and empires collapse in much the same way.

Before ancient Israel was suddenly conquered by the Babylonian Empire, the leaders and the people of Israel made thousands of bad decisions that gradually mired them in a lifestyle of idolatry, immorality, and rebellion. Before the sudden sack of Rome by the Visigoths in 410, Roman emperors and the Roman people made thousands of bad decisions that weakened and undermined the nation. Today, we are witnessing the gradual moral and spiritual bankruptcy of America. Unless we change our present course, a day will certainly come when the nation collapses—suddenly and catastrophically. And that may be just the opportunity for radical, fundamentalist Islam to take power.

By 2050, the United States of America and the rest of Western civilization may be swept away and replaced by an Islamic caliphate—not because the Islamists are stronger, smarter, or better armed than we are. If we lose our civilization, it will be because (as Lincoln prophetically pondered) we have hollowed out our civilization through immorality and the abandonment of faith in God.

But the death of our culture is not inevitable. We get to decide: Shall we remain free by coming to our senses both morally and spiritually? Or will we continue to participate in the slow, sure death of our civilization—death by cultural suicide?

Is the tide beginning to turn?

In June 2013, 30 million people rose up across Egypt and demanded an end to Islamist rule. They had suffered for a year under the authoritarian rule of Egyptian president Mohamed Morsi, an Islamist with ties to the Muslim Brotherhood. Egypt's Christian minority, about 10 million people, had been severely persecuted under Morsi, yet they had courageously defied threats from Islamist street gangs, attending all-night prayer meetings, asking God for deliverance. As a sea of protesters jammed Cairo's Tahrir Square, a military coalition, headed by General Abdel Fattah el-Sisi, removed Morsi from office.

General el-Sisi took the reins of government—much to the dismay of President Barack Obama and other Western leaders. Though el-Sisi wasn't democratically elected, he was not a self-aggrandizing dictator. He used his power on behalf of all the people of Egypt. Western leaders who opposed el-Sisi couldn't understand what a miraculous thing had taken place: A democratically minded reformer had come to power in an undemocratic way.

General el-Sisi proceeded to clean house, outlawing the Muslim Brotherhood and protecting the Christian minority from persecution. The Muslim Brotherhood retaliated by targeting Christians and burning their churches, homes, and businesses. It was the last gasp of the Brotherhood's vengeance as they realized their power was slipping away.

In 2014, el-Sisi ran for president in a fair and open election and won by a landslide. One of his first official acts as the democratically elected president was to begin rebuilding the eighty-five Christian churches that had been destroyed by the Muslim Brotherhood.

On November 1, 2017, I was in Egypt with a delegation of Christian pastors, leaders, and commentators. We met at the presidential palace in Cairo with President el-Sisi.

President el-Sisi is a soft-spoken man and one of the humblest leaders I've ever met. His nation faces many problems, but he handles them with extraordinary grace. He understands the danger of political Islam, he does not feel beholden to political correctness, and the leaders of the United States and Europe would do well to listen to him.

The meeting was supposed to last an hour, but the president graciously invited us to stay for three hours—he did not want us to stop asking questions and discussing the issues. Though President el-Sisi's English is flawless, he spoke in Arabic through a translator, probably to ensure that the official transcript could not be mistranslated and misconstrued. He warmly expressed his gratitude for our visit, and at one point he looked at me and said in Arabic, "You understand this without a translator."

"About 80 percent of it," I replied. Then, with tears in my eyes, I told him, "Mr. President, I believe you are God's gift not only to Egypt, but to the world. I watched you from my home in Atlanta on Christmas Eve 2015 when you visited the Coptic Cathedral in Cairo. I was moved by your promise to rebuild the churches that were destroyed by the Muslim Brotherhood. You kept your word and rebuilt them better than they were before. We're here to encourage you, support you, and thank you for saving Egypt from the Islamists."

At one point, President el-Sisi said to me, "Dr. Youssef, can you explain to me why President Obama did not follow our example and declare the Muslim Brotherhood to be a terrorist organization?"

"Mr. President," I said, "we have had pro-Islamists in the White House and in the State Department, giving advice to our leaders on foreign policy."

I was thinking of people like Dalia Mogahed, one of President Obama's advisers on Muslim affairs, who stated that "the majority of women around the world associate gender justice, or justice for women, with Sharia compliance,"[3] and Mohamed Elibiary, who had been mentored by convicted Hamas financier Shukri Abu Baker and who was appointed by President Obama to the Homeland Security Advisory Council.[4] I added, "I sincerely hope and pray that the current administration will not listen to advice from Islamist advisors."

President el-Sisi is a devout Muslim who has done everything he can to purge the Muslim Brotherhood from his government. He is living proof that there are Muslims who are not extremists, who are not Islamists, but who truly understand the threat that political Islam poses to the world. President el-Sisi has stated his goal of modernizing Islam, and he has called for a revolution within Islam to cleanse it of intolerance and violence. He understands that Islam is widely perceived to be a religion of the sword—and he wants Islam to become what it often *claims* to be—namely, a religion of peace.

I admire President el-Sisi for defending the Christian minority in Egypt and for removing Islamist elements from his government. I pray he comes to know Jesus as the only Way, the Truth, and the Life. I grew up among Muslims, and I love them dearly.

Moreover, God loves the Muslims and sent his Son to die on the cross for their salvation, just as he did for you and me. Across the Islamic world, thousands of Muslims are becoming disillusioned with the meaninglessness of the Muslim rituals and with the violence and extremism that is so common in the Muslim world. Many want to know more about Jesus.

We live in perilous times, the time of the Third Jihad, a time when Islam is advancing and Western civilization is retreating. But this is no time to despair. The age of the Third Jihad is also an age of opportunity for the gospel of Jesus Christ.

From fear of death to fearless living

Let me tell you about an Egyptian teenager. For her safety, I'll call her Fatima. Raised in a strict fundamentalist Muslim family, Fatima struggled intensely with depression and anxiety. She went to doctors who prescribed various medications, but nothing seemed to help. Her problem was not medical or psychological. Her problem was spiritual.

She recalled, "I was crying. I wanted to know the truth about God. I prayed, 'God, if you really exist—whether you are the God of the Bible or Allah of the Koran—please show me the way.'"

God heard her prayer—and he answered her.

One night, Fatima dreamed she was in a Christian church—a place she had never seen before. When she awoke, she had a feeling she had dreamed of a *real* church, though she had no idea where it might be. Could she find it? If so, could the people at the church help her find the answers she was looking for?

The next day, she asked around, describing the church she had seen in her dream.

"Have you ever seen or heard of a church like that?" she asked.

Finally, one person said, "Yes, I know of such a church. It's in a city on the coast."

Fatima traveled to the coastal city and went to the location where she had been told the church would be. And there it was, exactly as it had appeared in her dream. After taking a picture of the church with her phone, she walked inside and sat down. She was alone and began praying aloud, asking God to reveal himself to her.

Outside, the Muslim call to prayer echoed from the mosque down the street, filling Fatima with doubt.

Am I wrong to be here? she wondered.

Yet she'd been drawn to the church by a dream. Surely, only the true, living God could have sent her that dream.

That evening, Fatima went home and tried to practice the Muslim ritual of prayer. Praying to Allah brought no relief. In fact, she felt that the Muslim religion was suffocating her. With tears rolling down her face, she implored God, "Show me! If you exist, show me that you're real."

Fatima began reading the Old Testament, but it was hard for her to understand what it meant. She asked her Muslim friends what the Bible was about, but her friends were horrified at her interest in the "infidel" religion and told her to stop reading the Bible.

Her parents began to notice changes in her behavior and were curious. They sneaked a look at her phone and found the photo she had taken of the church in the coastal city. When they asked her about the picture, she confessed her doubts about Islam and her curiosity about Christianity.

Fatima's father flew into a rage and accused her of bringing shame on their family. He slapped her and beat her and locked her in her room. He ordered Fatima's mother not to allow Fatima any food until she came to her senses.

"But what if she doesn't change her mind?" her mother asked.

The father hinted darkly that an honor killing might be necessary.

Fatima languished for days, believing she had disgraced her family but still wanting to know the truth. Day after day, her parents demanded to know if she was ready to return to Islam. She honestly confessed that she still doubted.

Finally, her parents offered her an option: Her cousin was willing to marry her. He was a devout Muslim, and her parents believed that his strong faith would remove her doubts and draw her back into Islam. Fatima was horrified. If she went ahead with the marriage, she might never find the truth for herself.

Her parents arranged the date for the wedding. They watched her closely to make sure she went ahead with the plan. One day, when her parents left her unguarded, she escaped with little more than the clothes on her back and a Bible she had kept hidden.

During the time her parents had kept her locked up, Fatima had become convinced that the God of the Bible was the one true God and that Jesus Christ was God incarnate. That's all she knew. She knew nothing about how to receive him as the

Lord of her life. She needed someone to help her understand the good news of Jesus Christ.

Hiding in the home of a friend, she stayed up late one night watching satellite TV. She came across a Christian broadcast in Arabic that told her how to have peace with God through faith in Jesus Christ.

Best of all, there was an Egyptian phone number she could call to speak to a Christian counselor. When she called the number, she made contact with the follow-up team at Leading The Way (the international ministry I founded in 1988 as an evangelistic outreach to the Muslim world), and they helped her find a church and gave her Christian materials to read, including the Arabic edition of my book *Finding the Joy You've Always Wanted*. Soon after that, Fatima gave her life to Christ, and she's been growing as a Christian ever since.

Even though Fatima knew that her father had threatened an honor killing if she left the Islamic religion, she went back to tell her family about her faith in Christ, believing that God would protect her. When she talked to her family, they could tell that something was different about her—and she knew they sensed the presence of the Holy Spirit within her.

As I write these words, Fatima's parents are still committed Muslims, and they are still angry with her. But she talks to them, prays for them, and hopes she can love them into the Kingdom of God.

Eventually, she moved from Egypt to Lebanon—not out of fear of her parents, but because some Muslim coworkers had threatened to kill her. She received financial assistance from Help The Persecuted, another Leading The Way ministry, which allowed her to restart her life in a safe location. She still witnesses to her family through letters and phone calls.

"I used to be very scared of death," she says today, "but now I wish for it, because now I know that I have already gained eternal life. I'm not scared anymore."[5]

History repeats itself

We are living in amazing times. I have received many reports of Muslims who have dreamed dreams that have drawn them to the cross of Jesus. This is a great time for Christian believers to take a stand for the truth. This is a great time for Christians to be bold and unafraid as we face the future.

The days ahead may even be a time of great revival. That is what we need. That is what I pray for. We need revival in America. We need revival in Europe. We need revival in Africa, the Middle East, Asia, and all around the world.

One of the greatest revivals in history took place on both sides of the Atlantic during the 1730s and 1740s. Called the Evangelical Revival in Great Britain, it was led by George Whitefield and John Wesley. In the American colonies, a similar movement was called the Great Awakening, and God used a preacher named Jonathan Edwards to lead it.

The Great Awakening broke out in the Massachusetts town of Northampton. Like many pastors, Jonathan Edwards had labored faithfully for years, yet his sermons seemed not to penetrate the cold hearts in his congregation. Then one Sunday in 1734, half a dozen people gave professions of faith in Christ and were baptized. One was a young woman with a reputation for loose morals, and the change in her life was evident to all. Over the next six months, three hundred more souls were saved. The news and the joy in the Lord spread throughout the region. Soon revival broke out in towns and villages all around Massachusetts and in neighboring Pennsylvania. No one could have planned it or foreseen it. But Jonathan Edwards had prayed for it, and the Lord sent revival.

These leaders of the Great Awakening preached a pure and biblical gospel message that transcended denominational differences. They focused on the need for salvation by grace through faith in Jesus Christ. They made sure their congregations knew that conversion was not merely a mental assent to a doctrinal creed. It was a new birth that comes from a personal relationship with Jesus.

Alan Heimert, a longtime Harvard professor and the author of *Religion and the American Mind*, analyzed the history of the Great Awakening of the 1730s and 1740s alongside the history of the American Revolution of 1775 to 1783. He concluded that without revival there would have been no revolution. "The evangelical impulse," Heimert writes, "promoted almost entirely within the church . . . was the avatar and instrument of a fervent American nationalism."[6]

I firmly believe that the words of the Declaration of Independence—"We hold these truths to be self-evident, that all men are created equal, that they are endowed by their Creator with certain unalienable rights, that among these are life, liberty, and the pursuit of happiness"—could not have been written if the American revivalist preachers had not preached the words of Jesus: "If you hold to my teaching, you are really my disciples. Then you will know the truth, and the truth will set you free."[7] Liberty is not only one of the blessings of being an American, it's also one of the blessings of knowing Jesus Christ as our Lord and Savior.

Unless there is genuine revival throughout our civilization, we are going to lose our liberty. Look at history. Whenever the church lost its vision, its sense of biblical authority, its sense of urgency for preaching the uncompromised gospel of Jesus Christ, the result was a spiritual vacuum. When there is a spiritual vacuum, you can count on one thing: Something will rush in to fill it.

Today, there is a spiritual vacuum in Great Britain and Europe. Countless churches stand empty. What is rushing to fill that void? Islam. And not just moderate Islam. Political and militant Islam have become firmly entrenched in Great Britain and on the continent of Europe. The Islamists are demanding to be given the buildings of those dead churches so they can turn them into mosques. This is nothing new. We have seen this before. This is the pattern of Islamic conquest, the pattern of the First Jihad, the Second Jihad, and now the Third Jihad.

Historically, Islamic conquest always advanced most rapidly when the Christians and the churches in their path were morally and spiritually weak. Let me give you an example from the era of the First Jihad.

The weakening of the early church began in the second century, five hundred years before the birth of Muhammad. In Phrygia, a Roman province in Asia Minor (modern Turkey), a church cleric named Montanus founded a pseudo-Christian sect. His followers called it "the New Prophecy," but this heretical movement came to be known as Montanism, and it spread like an aggressive cancer throughout the church in the Roman Empire. Some churches wisely rejected the heresy of Montanus, others welcomed it, and some churches were torn apart by Montanist factions.

The essential heresy of Montanism is the claim that the Bible is not a closed canon and that prophets continue to speak with the authority of Scripture. Once a church decides that Scripture is no longer the final authority, it has opened Pandora's box—and an infinite array of heresies come spilling out.

Though Montanism eventually died out in most regions of the Roman Empire, tens of thousands of Christian churches across North Africa—in Morocco, Algeria, Tunisia, Libya, and Egypt—embraced the heresy. When the hordes of Islamic invaders rolled from Arabia across North Africa, they encountered thousands of Montanist churches—churches that were open to new doctrines and new revelations and that no longer believed that the Bible was God's final revealed word. When the Muslims told these churches, "We bring you a new message from Allah," many of these churches eagerly received the Muslim religion.

It didn't take long for Islam to conquer North Africa. Within three decades, all the North African churches had become mosques—except the Coptic Church in Egypt. Why did the Coptic Church survive when all the other North African churches succumbed to the onslaught of the Islamists? I believe it's because the Coptic Church, which was founded by Mark the Evangelist, held fast to the truth of Scripture and rejected the "new prophecies" of the Montanists.

Even today, we hear about churches that claim to offer new

prophetic revelations, but all they really offer is confusion. We must reject any so-called revelation that we have not already received in the Word of God. Tucked away in the epistle of Jude is a profound statement that we must never forget: "Contend for the faith that was once for all entrusted to God's holy people."[8] Contend for biblical faith! Fight for it, defend it, stand firm on it, add nothing new to it, and don't subtract anything from it.

There are many faithful churches that still preach the uncompromised, uncontaminated gospel of Jesus Christ. But many other churches have abandoned their evangelical roots, and many preachers now teach the false gospels of universalism, the social gospel, the prosperity gospel, the hypergrace gospel, or some other perversion of God's truth. False Christianity creates a vacuum that militant Islam is ready to fill.

Humanly speaking, there is no hope for the world. There is no strategy, no plan, no approach we can use to reverse the downward spiral of our civilization. It's hopeless. Our culture is too far gone, too steeped in secular values, too hostile to Jesus and his gospel of grace.

But have we given up? No. Nothing is too hard for the Lord. And he is still working through ordinary believers like you and me to affect the course of history. What can you and I do? What does God want to do through us to accomplish his eternal plan for human history?

The key to survival: revival

Jesus calls us to be salt and light in our culture. Salt is a preservative. Light illuminates. If we cease to be salt and light in our culture, it won't be long before our culture becomes corrupted and dark. We are already seeing signs of moral corruption and spiritual darkness engulfing our civilization.

The only hope we have of overcoming the Third Jihad is a genuine, churchwide revival. But we can't force revival to happen. We can't strategize our way to revival. Only the Holy Spirit can open hearts and bring about a reawakening in the church and a fresh awakening in our culture. I believe it was Stephen Olford who defined revival as "an invasion from heaven that brings a conscious awareness of God." Revival is nothing *we* do—it's something God does in us when we make ourselves prayerfully, obediently available for his invasion of our lives.

Here's an action agenda—a checklist of steps we can take to prepare ourselves to be invaded and used by God, so we can endure and have victory over the Third Jihad:

1. *Seek God's presence.* I once heard revival defined as "the church falling in love with Jesus all over again." That's a beautiful and fitting definition—not the entire definition, but a very good start. The apostle James writes, "Come near to God and he will come near to you."[9] If we want to experience the invasion of God's Spirit in our lives, we must lower our defenses, open the gates of our lives, and invite him in. We must want to be with him, to talk to him, to revel in his presence.

Jesus says in Revelation 3:20, "Here I am! I stand at the door and knock. If anyone hears my voice and opens the door, I will come in and eat with that person." People often quote this as an appeal to the unsaved to receive Jesus as Lord and Savior, and it's a very good verse for that purpose.

But in its original context, Jesus is speaking not to the unsaved, but to Christians in the church at Laodicea. Of the seven churches mentioned in Revelation, Laodicea was the church most like the Western church today—a complacent, lukewarm church about which Jesus says, "Because you are lukewarm—neither hot nor cold—I am about to spit you out of my mouth."[10] It was a church that thought itself rich and prosperous but was truly "wretched, pitiful, poor, blind, and naked."[11] It was, Jesus says, a church in need of "gold refined in the fire,"[12] a church in need of revival.

Jesus stands at the door of our lives, the door of our churches, and he knocks. Listen for his voice, open the door, invite him in to spend time with you, to have a heart-to-heart conversation with you, to share a meal with you—and he will come in. Fall in love with Jesus all over again. If you do, he will commune with you, and he will revive you.

2. *Devote yourself to God's Word.* The psalmist David writes, "The law of the LORD is perfect, refreshing the soul."[13] If you want to experience revival from God, then drink deeply from the Word of God. Jesus said that living in the Word is the key to a victorious life in him: "If you remain in me and my words remain in you, ask whatever you wish, and it will be done for you."[14] Read God's Word, study it, memorize it, meditate on it, and build its truth into your life.

Everywhere I go, I see people staring at their phones. Their heads are bowed, as if in prayer, and the phone casts a radiant glow on their faces. Am I describing you? Is that how you spend much of your day? What if, instead of checking Facebook or playing Minecraft, you were meditating on God's Word using a Bible app? What if you used your phone to learn memory verses or to read a chapter a day from the Psalms or the Gospel of John?

Do you have a plan for reading God's Word every day? Do you have a daily routine for spending time in the Bible? Do you read the Bible to increase your head knowledge—or to change your life? What are some time-wasting habits you could break to make more time for God's Word? If you want revival in your life, you must have the Bible in your life. The Bible is the key that unlocks the door to revival. The healing of our land will begin with the habitual study and bold proclamation of God's Word.

3. *Deal with sin—and have a hunger for righteousness.* Salvation Army missionary Gipsy Smith was one of the greatest revival preachers of the early twentieth century. When a man asked him the secret to experiencing revival in the church, Smith replied, "Go home and take a piece of chalk. Draw a circle around yourself. Then pray, 'O Lord, revive everything inside this circle.'"[15] Revival in the church begins with revival in each individual believer. We start with ourselves and deal with the sin in our lives. Once we have confessed and repented of our sin, we go forth with a genuine, heartfelt hunger for righteousness in our lives.

But we don't like to face the sin in our lives, do we? We don't like to let go of our sinful habits and false pride. Instead, we pray for revival with unrepentant hearts and unconfessed sin in our lives. We are like King Saul, who made all the right sacrifices but disobeyed God's commands. The prophet Samuel confronted Saul's disobedience, saying, "Does the LORD delight in burnt offerings and sacrifices as much as in obeying the LORD? To obey is better than sacrifice, and to heed is better than the fat of rams."[16] About this verse, A. W. Tozer once observed:

> Have you noticed how much praying for revival has been going on of late—and how little revival has resulted? . . .
>
> I believe our problem is that we have been trying to substitute praying for obeying; and it simply will not work. . . .
>
> Prayer is never an acceptable substitute for obedience. The sovereign Lord accepts no offering from His creatures that is not accompanied by obedience. To pray for revival while ignoring or actually flouting the plain precept laid down in the Scriptures is to waste a lot of words and get nothing for our trouble.[17]

If you want the Spirit of Almighty God to come into your life and revive your spirit and use you in a mighty way, begin with confession and repentance from sin. God has promised that he will live with those who are humble and he will revive those who are sorry for their sins:

> This is what the high and exalted One says—
>   he who lives forever, whose name is holy:
> "I live in a high and holy place,
>   but also with the one who is contrite and lowly
>   in spirit,
> to revive the spirit of the lowly
>   and to revive the heart of the contrite."[18]

If we want to experience the invasion of God's reviving Spirit, we must pray with the psalmist, "Search me, God, and know my heart; test me and know my anxious thoughts. See if there is any offensive way in me, and lead me in the way everlasting."[19]

4. *Be constant in worship.* If you want a blueprint for joy in your life, if you want a formula for revival in your church, then assemble together in sincere worship with fellow believers. God didn't design us to go it alone in this world. He designed his church to be a community of brothers and sisters who share their lives together. Jesus said that when believers assemble to unite their hearts in worship, a miracle takes place: "For where two or three gather in my name, there am I with them."[20]

We hear people around us say, "I don't need to worship God in church. I can worship him anywhere," or "Churches are full of hypocrites," or some other excuse. Yes, we can worship God wherever we find ourselves, and we should. And yes, there's no shortage of hypocrites in the church—but for every hypocrite in a sound, Bible-preaching church, you will find a dozen, if not a hundred, people who are God's gracious gift to the world, who exemplify the love of Christ to everyone they meet.

The church wasn't invented by a committee of apostles. The church was invented by God himself. It was built by the Lord Jesus Christ. After Simon confessed that Jesus is "the Messiah, the Son of the living God," Jesus gave Simon a new name—Peter (which means *rock*)—and said, "On this rock I will build my church, and the gates of Hades will not overcome it."[21]

Jesus has built, and continues to build, his church on the solid rock of the truth uttered by Peter, that Jesus is the Messiah, the Son of the living God. If we ignore or despise the church, we ignore or despise what Jesus himself has built. If we want to experience revival, we must assemble with other believers, because revival always takes place in communities of faith. Revival doesn't happen in isolation. It's a shared experience. It happens when the Spirit of God invades a body of believers who have prepared their hearts and opened themselves up to him.

When revival comes to a church, the news spreads quickly. As evangelist Leonard Ravenhill once said, "You never have to advertise a fire. Everyone comes running when there's a fire. Likewise, if your church is on fire, you will not have to advertise it. The community will already know it."[22]

5. *Pray for revival.* Nineteenth-century South African preacher Andrew Murray writes, "The coming revival must begin with a great prayer revival. It is in the closet, with the door shut, that the sound of abundance of rain will be first heard. An increase of secret prayer . . . will be the sure harbinger of blessing."[23]

After King Solomon completed construction of the great Temple in Jerusalem and dedicated it with prayer, the Lord appeared to him at night and said:

I have heard your prayer and have chosen this place for myself as a temple for sacrifices.

When I shut up the heavens so that there is no rain, or command locusts to devour the land or send a plague among my people, if my people, who are called by my name, will humble themselves and pray and seek my face and turn from their wicked ways, then I will hear from heaven, and I will forgive their sin and will heal their land.[24]

That's an amazing promise—and it comes with a prediction: There will be dark days ahead. God says, "*When* I shut up the heavens so that there is no rain, or command locusts to devour the land or send a plague among my people." Not *if*—*when*. When a believer or a church or a nation turns away from God, God must sometimes send trials and sufferings to get their attention. He may even command a plague of jihadists to come against us like locusts to devour the land.

What can save us when that day comes? Revival—which comes when we call upon God in prayer. If we who bear the name of Christ will humble ourselves and pray and seek his face and turn from our wicked ways, then he will hear from heaven and he will forgive our sin—*and will heal our land.*[25]

When the First Jihad came to North Africa, the armies of Islam devoured the churches from Morocco to Libya—but the church in Egypt, the Coptic Church, survived. The Egyptian churches lived in God's presence, held fast to God's Word, cleansed themselves of sin, hungered for righteousness, devoted themselves to worship, and earnestly prayed—and revival became their survival. The Islamists could not destroy them or intimidate them or convert them out of their faith.

Thirteen centuries later, when the Muslim Brotherhood came to power in Egypt, led by an Islamist named Mohamed Morsi, Egypt's oppressed Christian minority prayed day and night for deliverance. They experienced a revival that blessed the entire nation and tossed the Muslim Brotherhood out of power in Egypt. Those Coptic brothers and sisters in Christ are an example to you and me of how we are to respond to the Islamists and the Third Jihad.

We are to respond with prayer, humbly inviting God to revive us and to heal our land. Our prayer is that of the psalmist who writes, "Will you not revive us again, that your people may rejoice in you?"[26]

Western civilization will not stand against the Third Jihad unless God brings revival to his church in the West. With my own eyes, I have seen revival breaking out in parts of Asia and even in Indonesia, the most populous Muslim nation on earth. I praise God for the way his Spirit is moving in many parts of the world. But we desperately need revival in the West—in America, the United Kingdom, and Europe. We need an invasion of the Spirit of God—before a very different kind of invasion becomes inevitable.

The key to our survival is revival.

12

DON'T BE AFRAID

THE THIRD JIHAD is being waged against our civilization through violent attacks by militant Muslims and cultural subversion by political Muslims. But the Third Jihad is also being waged against the church as spiritual warfare—a jihad of fear and falsehood designed to paralyze and neutralize Christians and diminish our effectiveness for God. Satan wants to strike fear into our hearts. Satan wants us to be afraid to share our faith with Muslims, afraid to speak God's truth lest we offend someone, and afraid of being labeled *Islamophobes*. If Satan can immobilize us through fear, he will win the spiritual battle.

As we discussed in chapter 6, Winston Churchill understood that the retreat of Islamic imperialism at the end of the nineteenth century was only a temporary situation. In time, he predicted, the "militant and proselytizing" forces of political

Islam would regather their strength and come roaring back to threaten Western civilization.[1] Historian Hilaire Belloc understood that not only would political Islam rise again, but it had never truly departed, despite the fall of the Ottoman empire. Belloc predicted that militant Islam was destined to "reappear again as the prime enemy of our civilization."[2]

The violent jihad of the militant terrorists and the gradual jihad of the political Islamists are real, and both threaten our civilization. But we, as followers of Christ, must not be deceived or distracted by the military wars, the terror wars, or the political wars being waged all around us by the warriors of jihad. For Christians, the *real* battlefield is *spiritual*. The *real* jihad is a battle for the control of our wills, our minds, our emotions, our souls. The real enemy, the real terrorist, the most dangerous jihadist we face is Satan himself, and if he can immobilize us with terror, he wins.

God has not given us a spirit of fear. He has given us the Spirit of power, the Spirit of love, the Spirit of a disciplined mind.[3] He has given us everything we need to win the spiritual battle against Satan, the ultimate terrorist.

Mark Thompson was the director-general of the British Broadcasting Corporation from 2004 to 2012. He is currently CEO of the New York Times Company. In February 2012, as he prepared to step down as head of the BBC, Thompson gave an interview for Oxford University's Free Speech Debate, in which he made a shocking admission: Under his leadership, the BBC had treated Muslims with deference while reserving harsher criticism for Christians.[4]

Why?

Fear!

Christianity, he said, is "a broad-shouldered religion."[5] In other words, Christians would graciously endure having their faith criticized, defamed, or mocked—which happened regularly on BBC programming. Christians might make phone calls or send emails of complaint. BBC producers had no fear of phone calls and emails—but they were very much afraid of threats from offended Muslims.

"Without question," Thompson said, "'I complain in the strongest possible terms' is different from 'I complain in the strongest possible terms and I am loading my AK47 as I write.' This definitely raises the stakes."[6]

This is how the Third Jihad is being waged in the West today—not just by violence, but by fear and intimidation. And it's working. In the face of Islamist intimidation, the BBC folded like a cheap suit.

And so it goes across the United Kingdom, Europe, and America. For decades, throughout Western civilization, and even in America—the land of the First Amendment—secularists have been aggressively pushing every remnant of Christianity out of the public square, off the public airwaves, out of the public schools, out of sight and out of mind. The thinking of the secularists is so skewed that they even use the First Amendment, which grants us freedom of religion and speech, to *silence* Christians. They say, "We have freedom *from* religion here! I don't have to listen to your religious speech. You can't talk about Jesus or wear a cross or read your Bible in a school or on any other government property because that would be establishing a state religion!" It's insanity, but that's the logic of the secularists for you.

But the insanity doesn't end with silencing Christians.

When the Islamists come to America, what do the secularists say? "Come right in! How can we accommodate you? Would you like to teach our schoolchildren about Islam? Go right ahead. Would you like to deliver the opening prayer for Congress? Become an advisor to the president? Help shape American foreign policy? Be our guest!"

One reason the secularists are so accommodating to the Islamists is fear. Most Westerners are afraid of offending the Islamists, and that goes double for Western secularists.

Fear works. Fear is especially effective against those with shallow moral and spiritual roots. If you have shallow roots, you won't be planted firmly when the winds of opposition come. You'll be easily plucked up and blown away.

But if you have a strong faith in God, you will have roots that are planted deeply in the earth. You'll be strong and immovable, even against hurricane-force persecution.

Faith in God makes us fearless. God has promised to be our shield and fortress. Deuteronomy 3:22 emboldens us, saying, "Do not be afraid of them; the LORD your God himself will fight for you." God is not remote and uninvolved. He goes before us, fighting our battles.

When Joshua was preparing to lead the people of Israel into the Promised Land, the Lord came to him and said:

Moses my servant is dead. Now then, you and all these people, get ready to cross the Jordan River into the land I am about to give to them—to the Israelites. I will give you every place where you set your foot, as I promised

Moses. Your territory will extend from the desert to Lebanon, and from the great river, the Euphrates—all the Hittite country—to the Mediterranean Sea in the west. No one will be able to stand against you all the days of your life. As I was with Moses, so I will be with you; I will never leave you nor forsake you. Be strong and courageous, because you will lead these people to inherit the land I swore to their ancestors to give them.

Be strong and very courageous. Be careful to obey all the law my servant Moses gave you; do not turn from it to the right or to the left, that you may be successful wherever you go. Keep this Book of the Law always on your lips; meditate on it day and night, so that you may be careful to do everything written in it. Then you will be prosperous and successful. Have I not commanded you? Be strong and courageous. Do not be afraid; do not be discouraged, for the LORD your God will be with you wherever you go.[7]

Five times in these two paragraphs, God says to Joshua, "Be strong and courageous" or "Do not be afraid" or "Do not be discouraged." Five times! God clearly wanted Joshua to get the message: *Don't be afraid, Joshua—be fearless, because I, the Lord, am with you.* And God wants the same message to sink in with you and me. That's why he tells us so often in Scripture, in various ways: *Don't be afraid!*

We hear God's message of encouragement from the psalmists: "The LORD is with me; I will not be afraid. What can mere mortals do to me?"[8] We hear this same message from the prophet Isaiah: "This is what the LORD says—he who created you, Jacob, he who formed you, Israel: 'Do not fear, for I have redeemed you; I have summoned you by name; you are mine."[9] We hear this same message from Jesus himself: "Peace I leave with you; my peace I give you. I do not give to you as the world gives. Do not let your hearts be troubled and do not be afraid."[10] We hear the same message expressed by the apostle Paul: "The Spirit God gave us does not make us timid, but gives us power, love and self-discipline."[11]

Please understand, it's not a sin to experience fear. Our feelings are natural responses to the good and bad things that happen to us. It's perfectly normal to be afraid in a threatening situation—an intruder in the house, a health crisis or injury, or a financial setback. God gave us the emotion of fear to protect us and to motivate us to deal with the threat by either standing up to it or fleeing it. Never feel guilty for feeling afraid.

But at the same time, never give in to fear. Never let fear control you. Never let fear overwhelm your faith. When the Bible tells us that God has not given us a spirit of timidity and fear, it means that *fearfulness is not our natural state*. Yes, we will be afraid from time to time, but God gives us the power to respond to fear through an awareness of God's love and self-disciplined thinking. And as the apostle John reminds us, "There is no fear in love. But perfect love drives out fear."[12]

Life is too short and eternity too long to waste a single moment controlled by fear. Say "no!" to your fears. Live boldly and courageously for Christ, because the rewards for those who overcome their fears and serve him courageously will last for all eternity. Focus on God's presence and his promise to always be with you.[13] Focus on the power of God and his promise to fight for you. Focus on the love of God and his promise to never leave you or forsake you.[14]

Don't let your heart be troubled, and don't be afraid.[15]

Be strong and courageous as you stand for the truth, as you graciously profess your faith in Jesus before your friends, neighbors, coworkers, employers, teachers, fellow students, and everyone else in your life. Be strong and courageous as you stand before the school board, the city council, the student council, the courtroom, or wherever God calls you to make a public stand for his truth. Be strong and courageous as you witness to the truth on social media, in lunchroom conversations, and over the back fence.

Above all, be strong and courageous when sharing your faith in Jesus with your Muslim friends and neighbors. Pray that the Muslims within your sphere of influence would see Jesus in your life. Be strong and courageous, but also patient and kind, when talking to Muslims. Don't become angry or argumentative. Don't try to win a debate. Remember the wise counsel of the apostle Paul: "The god of this age has blinded the minds of unbelievers, so that they cannot see the light of the gospel that displays the glory of Christ, who is the image of God."[16]

Become acquainted with the teachings of the Koran. Tell your Muslim friends that you know Muslims respect Jesus as a miracle worker and that the Koran teaches that he was born of a virgin and lived a sinless life. The biggest difference between what the Koran and the Bible teach about Jesus is that the

Koran denies that Jesus died on the cross and rose from the dead. To Muslims, Jesus is a dead prophet; but to Christians, he is the resurrected Lord.

Don't be timid—speak candidly about the essential elements of the Christian faith: Jesus died on the cross for our sins, he was dead and buried, he was raised on the third day, he ascended into heaven, and he is coming again. Muslims believe the Bible has been corrupted and may tell you so. Without arguing, simply state that you have always found the Bible to be internally consistent and reliable.

Ask your Muslim friend a great soul-winner's question: "If you were to die tonight, do you know for certain that you would go to heaven?" Most Muslims would have to answer *no*. This will give you an opening to share your faith.

We cannot defend our faith and defeat the Islamists with the weaponry of this world. This is not to say that Western nations shouldn't protect innocent populations, defend their homelands against attack, and wage war against ISIS and other terrorist groups. We should and we must. That is what God ordained governments to do.[17]

But we in the church of Jesus Christ are not fighting the War on Terror. We are fighting a different battle. And in this battle, the Muslims are not our enemy. Even the jihadists are not our enemy in this war. Our battle is a *spiritual* battle—not against the jihadists themselves, but against the evil spiritual forces that use the jihadists to do their bidding. As the apostle Paul reminded the Christians in Ephesus, "Our struggle is not against flesh and blood, but against the rulers, against the authorities, against the powers of this dark world and against the spiritual forces of evil in the heavenly realms."[18] Paul goes on to describe the spiritual weaponry available to us.

First, we are to put on "the belt of truth."[19] This includes God's truth as revealed in the Bible and also includes a commitment to always speak the truth in love, being honest and open about our faith, being committed to never using falsehood to our advantage, and never spreading Internet rumors or fake news because we think it will help our side. All truth is God's truth, and all lies belong to Satan, "the father of lies."[20]

Second, we are to wear "the breastplate of righteousness."[21] Today we would refer to a breastplate as a flak jacket or a bullet-proof vest. We can protect ourselves from satanic attack by keeping ourselves morally pure, immediately confessing and repenting of sin, and maintaining a godly and righteous heart.

Third, we are to have our "feet fitted with the readiness that comes with the gospel of peace."[22] In other words, we're to be always prepared to share the good news of Jesus Christ with everyone we meet, including our Muslim neighbors. Through Jesus, we have peace with God and with one another.

Fourth, we are to take up "the shield of faith"[23] by keeping our hopes and expectations focused on the Lord. When the evil one flings fiery arrows of temptation or discouragement or adversity at us, we keep our eyes steadfastly on Jesus.

Fifth, we are to put on "the helmet of salvation,"[24] which encases the head, protecting our minds from the lies of this world; from the filth that is so prevalent in the entertainment media and on the Internet; from the propaganda that fills our news media; and from the anti-Christian indoctrination of our public schools and universities. We are saved by grace through faith, and the knowledge of our salvation protects our minds from the enemy's attempts to corrupt our thoughts with worldly ideas and doubts.

Sixth, we are to wield "the sword of the Spirit, which is the word of God."[25] The greatest source of error and weakness in the church is ignorance or abuse of God's Word. Islam itself is largely the result of Muhammad's misunderstanding of the truth of God's Word revealed in both the Old and New Testaments. If we neglect to study God's Word, we leave ourselves wide open to deception and heretical ideas promoted by false teachers. There is no more effective weapon in our spiritual arsenal than the sword of God's Spirit—that is, the truth of the Bible.

Pray daily for your Muslim friends. Ask God to open their eyes and soften their hearts so that they can discover Jesus not merely as a miracle-working prophet named Isa, but as their living Lord, Savior, and friend. Ask God to fill them with a deep hunger to know more about our risen Lord. Pray for wisdom and boldness to share God's truth with the Muslims around you.

Pray especially often for them during the Islamic month of Ramadan, when Muslims fast to receive forgiveness from Allah. Muslims believe that the Koran was revealed to Muhammad during the month of Ramadan, and many devout Muslims are spiritually open during this time because they hope to receive a dream or revelation from Allah. Though Satan often uses Ramadan as a time of delusion and deception for Muslims, this is also a time when God can reach the hearts of receptive Muslims to reveal his truth.

Pray for Muslims who have left Islam and have given their

lives to Jesus. The pressure of living as a Christian in an Islamic culture is beyond imagination. Those who leave Islam are often shunned by family members, attacked by former friends, interrogated by the police, and violently persecuted. Some have been murdered. Pray that God will protect them, encourage them, and surround them with an awareness of his presence.

Let me leave you with a letter we received from a young man in Libya who has been watching our evangelistic programming on THE KINGDOM SAT, the 24-7 satellite channel operated by Leading The Way. We receive calls, emails, and letters like this one every day:

Hello,
I really do not know how to start. Should I cry, asking for help? I'm from Libya. I'm nineteen years old, from a Muslim family.

Ever since I was a little boy, I was attracted to Christianity. At the age of seventeen, I made a decision to believe in Christ. I drew a cross on my chest, specifically on my heart, and I drew another cross on my bed. Whenever I see a cross, my heart beats hard, a feeling I do not know how to describe to you. It is a very spiritual feeling.

I thought of talking to Christians so that they could tell me more about being a Christian, but it's very difficult because there are almost no Christians around me. I haven't seen any Libyan Christians in my life.

I'm writing to you while tears are running down my face—tears of joy when I remember what happened to me. I was watching TV when I accidentally found some

Christian channels. I couldn't believe my eyes! This was the most joyous moment of my life. I watched these channels late at night, after everyone else in my family went to bed.

Among these channels was AL MALAKOOT SAT [THE KINGDOM SAT]. And that is why I want to communicate with you today. Please help me learn about Christianity. How can I tell people I am a Christian without being rejected? If I said to my family, "I am a Christian," do you know what they would do? They would hate me. They would punish me. And they might hand me over to an Islamic group to torture me. O God, help me!

I hope with all my heart that you can help me find a way to tell my family. What if they hate me? What if they punish me? If they do, let it be because of Jesus, who came with his light into my heart.

I hope you can answer me fast, but if you are unable to help me, please send my message to someone who can.

Our follow-up team reached out to this young man and have begun to help him—even as I write these words.

Meanwhile, the threat of the Third Jihad is real and it is coming—but praise God, he is stronger and more real than the jihadist threat. Amid all the bad news coming out of the Muslim world, there is good news from people like this young man in Libya, people who are being called out of Islam and into the Kingdom of Christ.

I hope you will pray for this young man and for the entire Muslim world. Pray that the hearts and minds of the Muslim people will open up and be receptive to the gospel of Jesus

Christ. Pray for opportunities to be God's messenger of peace and hope and the good news of salvation to the Muslims around you. Pray for boldness to speak God's truth without compromise, in a spirit of Christlike love and humility.

Stand firm against the Third Jihad. Be bold and courageous. The Lord stands with you, and he will fight your battles.

Do not be afraid.

DISCUSSION QUESTIONS

CHAPTER 1: THE ISLAMIC STATES OF AMERICA

1. Do you think it's possible for the US, Mexico, and Canada to one day become the Islamic State of North America? Why or why not?

2. What factors in our society today would make an Islamic State of North America impossible or unlikely? What factors would make it possible?

3. What can we do to prevent an eventual Islamic State of North America?

CHAPTER 2: A CENTURIES-OLD WAR

1. George Washington responded to the Islamic threat in the Mediterranean by signing into law the Naval Act of 1794, which established the US Navy and provided for the building of six ships to protect American commerce overseas. Only three of those ships were eventually built.

When John Adams became president, he authorized further tribute payments to the Barbary states. When Thomas Jefferson became president, he stopped the tribute payments and sent the US Navy and US Marines to attack the Barbary states. Discuss these different approaches to state-sponsored terrorism. What parallels do you see to our situation today with Islamic terrorism? What differences do you see?

2. Ultimately, a buildup of military strength by the United States and European nations shifted the balance of power in the Mediterranean. How is military power a factor, or not a factor, in today's War on Terror?

CHAPTER 3: AT WAR—AND UNAWARE

1. According to journalist Lara Logan, Islamic terrorists and jihadists she has met over the years have told her that Islam is a *civilization*, not a *religion*. Why is this distinction important (especially in the United States), and how does it affect our response to the Islamists?

2. The word *Islam* means "submission" or "surrender." What differences, if any, are there between the surrender that Jesus Christ calls us to and the surrender that Islam demands?

CHAPTER 4: THE FIRST JIHAD

1. How much did you know, before reading this chapter, about the history of Islam, the First Jihad, and the spread of Islam

throughout the world? How does this historical information affect your views of Islam and Muslims today?

2. What parallels or differences do you see between the early days of Islam, the First Jihad, and Islam in the twenty-first century?

CHAPTER 5: A DISASTROUS RESPONSE

1. Based on your understanding of Christian history, were the Crusades primarily religious wars or political wars? Explain. From a biblical perspective, were the Crusades justified or unjustified? Why?

2. How would you respond to someone who challenges your Christian faith by saying, "What about the Crusades? What about the murder and torture committed by people who followed the same Jesus you're preaching to me?"

3. What can we learn from the example of Francis of Assisi about how we should approach Muslims in our day and age?

CHAPTER 6: THE SECOND JIHAD

1. How did the Second Jihad contribute to the rise of modern Western civilization?

2. How might God work to bring good from Islamic terrorism in our day?

3. What role can Christians play in resisting the spread of jihad across the world?

CHAPTER 7: THE THIRD JIHAD HAS BEGUN

1. From what you have read and heard, what motivates Muslims who pursue martyrdom? What differences do you see between Islamic martyrdom and Christian martyrdom?

2. If Western notions of freedom, human rights, and democracy are incompatible with Islam, how can these two worldviews coexist? What can we in the West do to preserve our civilization in the face of the Third Jihad?

3. Political Muslims are using the freedoms afforded them by Western political and legal systems to undermine and overthrow those same freedoms. What can we do to *preserve* our freedoms without violating our principles?

CHAPTER 8: THE THIRD JIHAD IN "EURABIA"

1. What lessons can we learn from the spread of the Third Jihad in France and Britain in recent years?

2. What similarities or differences between the United States and Europe would contribute to the success or failure of the Third Jihad in America?

3. What steps can be taken now in North America to ensure the safety of our political, legal, and social systems?

CHAPTER 9: COULD IT HAPPEN HERE?

1. According to former Assistant US Attorney Andrew McCarthy, *dawa* is "the advancement of the sharia agenda

through means other than violence and agents other than terrorists." What examples of *dawa* have you seen in our society in recent years?

2. Ayaan Hirsi Ali says that America's war on terror has failed because terror is not an enemy. Our enemy in the Third Jihad is the Islamist ideology. How can we effectively use truth to fight the Islamist agenda of *dawa* and *taqiya* (obscuring the truth)?

3. How should we respond to accusations of "intolerance" or "Islamaphobia" as we seek to preserve the values on which our nation was founded?

CHAPTER 10: THE SECULAR-ISLAMIST ALLIANCE

1. How are Islamists using the welfare state, liberal notions of multiculturalism, and liberal rules of political correctness to advance their agenda?

2. What is the difference between the idea of America as a "melting pot" and the more recent trend toward multiculturalism? How does multiculturalism differ from cultural diversity? Do you see multiculturalism as a threat to American democracy? Why or why not?

3. How does *underdogma*—"the liberal desire to support the underdog" by "correcting" power imbalances— compare to the biblical mandate to care for the poor and underprivileged? See, for example, Deuteronomy 15:10-11; Proverbs 14:31, 19:17, 22:9; 1 John 3:17-18.

CHAPTER 11: THE KEY TO SURVIVAL

1. If great civilizations commit suicide by becoming morally corrupt and spiritually indifferent, what practical steps and actions can we take to prevent this from happening in our nation?

2. Keeping in mind political differences between the United States and Egypt, what lessons can we learn from Egyptian president Abdel el-Sisi's response to the rise of Islamism in his country?

3. What can Christians do today to be "salt and light" in our culture?

CHAPTER 12: DON'T BE AFRAID

1. As part of the Third Jihad, Satan wants to strike fear in our hearts. What does the Bible tell us about how to effectively wage spiritual warfare?

2. How do we resist fear and intimidation in the face of the Third Jihad? How do we stand up for Christian values in our increasingly secularized society?

3. Read Psalm 46 and 1 Samuel 17:47. In practical terms, what does it mean to say, "The battle is the LORD's"? How does this affect our response to the Third Jihad?

ABOUT THE AUTHOR

MICHAEL YOUSSEF is the founder and president of Leading The Way with Dr. Michael Youssef, a worldwide ministry that leads the way for people living in spiritual darkness to discover the light of Christ through the creative use of media and on-the-ground ministry teams (www.LTW.org). His weekly television programs and daily radio programs are broadcast in twenty-five languages and seen worldwide, airing more than thirteen thousand times per week. He is also the founding pastor of The Church of The Apostles in Atlanta, Georgia.

Dr. Youssef was born in Egypt, but in 1984, he fulfilled a childhood dream of becoming an American citizen. He holds numerous degrees, including a PhD in social anthropology from Emory University. He has authored more than thirty-five books, including recent popular titles *The Barbarians Are Here* and *Jesus, Jihad and Peace*. He and his wife have four grown children and several grandchildren.

NOTES

CHAPTER 1: THE ISLAMIC STATES OF AMERICA

1. Ian Kershaw, "How Democracy Produced a Monster," *New York Times*, February 3, 2008, www.nytimes.com/2008/02/03/opinion/03iht-edkershaw .1.9700744.html.

2. Meira Svirsky, "As-Sabiqun/Masjid al-Islam," ClarionProject.org, April 7, 2013, https://clarionproject.org/sabiqun-masjid-al-islam.

3. Abdul Alim Musa, "Message to 2008 MSA-PSG Conference Attendees," Masjid Al-Islam, www.investigativeproject.org/documents/misc/472.pdf.

4. This quote has been variously attributed to science fiction writers Ray Bradbury (author of *Fahrenheit 451* and *The Martian Chronicles*) and Frank Herbert (author of *Dune*). For a discussion about who said it first, see https://quoteinvestigator.com/2010/10/19/prevent-the-future.

5. Bruce Bawer, *While Europe Slept: How Radical Islam Is Destroying the West from Within* (New York: Broadway Books, 2006), 16.

6. Ahmed Abdou Maher, "Why Don't Christians and Jews Accept Our Islam?," christian-dogma.com, March 1, 2018, www.christian-dogma.com/t1460860. Translated from Arabic by the author.

7. Ibid.

CHAPTER 2: A CENTURIES-OLD WAR

1. Jared Sparks, *The Writings of George Washington*, vol. ix (Boston: Russell, Odiorne, and Metcalf, 1835), 194.

2. Joseph Wheelan, *Jefferson's War: America's First War on Terror 1801–1805* (New York: Carroll & Graf, 2003), 7–8.

3. John Adams, letter to US Secretary of Foreign Affairs John Jay, February 17, 1786, in *The Works of John Adams*, vol. viii, ed. Charles Francis Adams (Boston: Little, Brown, 1853), 372.

4. Ibid, 372–373.

5. Ibid., 373.

6. John Adams and Thomas Jefferson, "American Peace Commissioners [letter] to John Jay, 28 March 1786." An image of the original handwritten letter can be found at www.loc.gov/resource/mtj1.005_0430_0433/?sp=2. A transcript of the letter can be found at https://founders.archives.gov/documents /Jefferson/01-09-02-0315.

7. Ibid.

8. Christopher Hitchens, "Jefferson Versus the Muslim Pirates," *City Journal,* Spring 2007, www.city-journal.org/html/jefferson-versus-muslim -pirates-13013.html.

9. Robert Davis, "British Slaves on the Barbary Coast," BBC.co.uk, February 17, 2011, www.bbc.co.uk/history/british/empire_seapower/white_slaves _01.shtml.

10. According to the Marine Corps Association and Foundation, "neither explanation has ever been verified." For more information, see "The Leatherneck Legacy" at www.mca-marines.org/leatherneck/leatherneck-legacy.

CHAPTER 3: AT WAR—AND UNAWARE

1. "Armstrong & Getty's Lara Logan Interview," The Armstrong and Getty Show podcast, August 8, 2018, www.iheart.com/podcast/The-Armstrong-and -Getty-Show-20474616/episode/armstrong-gettys-lara-logan -interview-29689893. Transcription by the author.

2. David Rose, "The Osama Files," *Vanity Fair,* June 4, 2007, www.vanityfair .com/news/2002/01/osama200201.

3. Janet McElligott, "Outside View: The One Who Got Away," United Press International, UPI Outside View commentary, July 6, 2004, www.upi.com /Outside-View-The-one-who-got-away/70991089093780.

4. Ibid.

5. *The 9/11 Commission Report,* National Commission on Terrorist Attacks Upon the United States of America, July 22, 2004, 110, www.9-11commission.gov /report/911Report.pdf.

6. Lawrence Wright, *The Looming Tower: Al-Qaeda and the Road to 9/11* (New York: Vintage, 2007), 251.

7. Osama bin Laden, interview with Peter Arnett, May 10, 1997, in Phil Hirschkorn, "Bin Laden the Focus of Embassy Bombing Trial," CNN.com, February 22, 2001, http://edition.cnn.com/2001/LAW/02/21/embassy .bombing.02/index.html.

8. PBS, "Frontline: Osama bin Laden v. the U.S.: Edicts and Statements," PBS.org, www.pbs.org/wgbh/pages/frontline/shows/binladen/who/edicts .html.

NOTES

CHAPTER 4: THE FIRST JIHAD

1. Abd al-Malik Ibn Hishām, *The Life of Muhammad, Apostle of Allah* (London: The Folio Society, 1964), 36.
2. Mark 16:15-16
3. John 18:36
4. Clifton Fadiman and André Bernard, eds., *Bartlett's Book of Anecdotes* (New York: Little, Brown, 2000), 417.
5. Hugh Kennedy, *The Great Arab Conquests: How the Spread of Islam Changed the World We Live In* (New York: Da Capo Press, 2007), 165.
6. Khalid Yahya Blankinship, *The End of the Jihad State: The Reign of Hisham Ibn 'Abd al-Malik and the Collapse of the Umayyads* (Albany: State University of New York Press, 1994), 37.
7. Edward Gibbon, *The History of the Decline and Fall of the Roman Empire*, vol. 6 (London: John Murray, 1887), 373.

CHAPTER 5: A DISASTROUS RESPONSE

1. Oliver J. Thatcher and Edgar Holmes McNeal, editors, *A Source Book for Medieval History* (New York: Scribners, 1905), www.gutenberg.org/files /42707/42707-h/42707-h.htm.
2. Edward H. Flannery, *The Anguish of the Jews: Twenty-Three Centuries of Antisemitism*, revised and updated edition (New York: Paulist Press, 2004), 92–93.
3. Michael D. Hull, "First Crusade: Siege of Jerusalem," *Military History*, June 1999, www.historynet.com/first-crusade-siege-of-jerusalem.htm.
4. Raymond d'Aguiliers, "Crusaders Capture Jerusalem," from *The Conquest of Jerusalem*, trans. August. C. Krey, modernized and abridged by Stephen Tomkins, ed. Dan Graves, ChristianHistoryInstitute.org, https://christianhistoryinstitute.org/study/module/crusaders.
5. Deuteronomy 12:31
6. Clifton Fadiman and André Bernard, eds., *Bartlett's Book of Anecdotes* (New York: Little, Brown, 2000), 215.
7. Excerpt of the *First Rule of Saint Francis*, chapter 16, trans. Paul Schwartz and Paul Lachance, in David Flood and Thaddée Matura, *The Birth of a Movement: A Study of the First Rule of St. Francis* (Chicago: Franciscan Herald Press, 1975), np.
8. Ibid.
9. Blake Neff, "Historicity & Holy War: Putting the Crusades in Context," *Dartmouth Apologia*, vol. 6, issue 1, Fall 2011, 29, https://issuu.com/apologia /docs/10_-_apologia1f.
10. Richard Dawkins, *The God Delusion* (New York: Houghton Mifflin, 2008), 349 ff. Dawkins makes this argument throughout chapter 9: "Childhood, Abuse and the Escape from Religion," see especially 366–367.

11. Ibid., 58.

12. Robert Louis Wilken, *The First Thousand Years: A Global History of Christianity* (New Haven: Yale University Press, 2012), 307–308.

CHAPTER 6: THE SECOND JIHAD

1. Rudi Paul Linder, *Nomads and Ottomans in Medieval Anatolia* (London: RoutledgeCurzon, 1997), 37.

2. Caroline Finkel, *Osman's Dream: The History of the Ottoman Empire* (New York: Basic Books, 2005), 5–6.

3. Paul Wittek, *The Rise of the Ottoman Empire: Studies in the History of Turkey, Thirteenth-Fifteenth Centuries* (New York: Routledge, 2012), 44.

4. Marios Philippides and Walter K. Hanak, *The Siege and Fall of Constantinople in 1453: Historiography, Topography, and Military Studies* (New York: Ashgate, 2011), 93.

5. Jonathan Phillips, *Holy Warriors: A Modern History of the Crusades* (New York: Random House, 2009), 300.

6. Steven Runciman, *The Fall of Constantinople 1453* (Cambridge, UK: Cambridge University Press, 1965), 152.

7. Lord Kinross, *The Ottoman Centuries: The Rise and Fall of the Turkish Empire* (New York: William Morrow, 1979), 115–116.

8. Marios Philippides and Walter K. Hanak, *The Siege and Fall of Constantinople in 1453: Historiography, Topography, and Military Studies* (New York: Ashgate Publishing, 2011), 253–254.

9. Gábor Ágoston and Bruce Masters, *Encyclopedia of the Ottoman Empire* (New York: Facts on File, 2009), 545.

10. Winston Spencer Churchill, *The River War*, first edition, vol. II (London: Longmans, Green, 1899), 249–250, https://archive.org/details/1899River WarVol2. Italics in the original. (This quote does not appear in the one -volume abridged edition of *The River War* published by Longmans, Green in 1902.)

11. Hilaire Belloc, *The Great Heresies* (Freeport, NY: Books for Libraries Press, 1938), 126–128, 130.

12. Bat Ye'or, *Islam and Dhimmitude: Where Civilizations Collide* (Cranbury, NJ: Associated University Presses, 2002), 199.

13. Robert Spencer, "Iraq: We Are Fighting for an Islamic State, Says Al-Qaeda in Iraq," *Jihad Watch*, October 19, 2005, www.jihadwatch.org/2005/10 /iraq-we-are-fighting-for-an-islamic-state-says-al-Qaeda-in-iraq.

CHAPTER 7: THE THIRD JIHAD HAS BEGUN

1. Niniek Karmini, Associated Press, "Neighbors Say Family That Bombed Churches Well Off, Friendly," FoxNews.com, www.foxnews.com/world/2018 /05/14/neighbors-say-family-that-bombed-churches-well-off-friendly.html.

2. Masrur Jamaluddin, Eliott C. McLaughlin and Susannah Cullinane, "Family of Suicide Bombers Attacks 3 Churches in Indonesia, Killing 12, Police Say," CNN.com, May 14, 2018, www.cnn.com/2018/05/13/asia/indonesia-church-attacks-surabaya/index.html.

3. Ibid.

4. Efraim Benmelech and Esteban F. Klor, "What Explains the Flow of Foreign Fighters to ISIS?" research paper, February 2018, https://scholars.huji.ac.il/sites/default/files/eklor/files/isis_february_14_2018.pdf.

5. Sayyid Qutb ash-Shaheed, "The America I Have Seen: In the Scale of Human Values" (1951), trans. Tarek Masoud and Ammar Fakeeh, https://archive.org/stream/SayyidQutb/The%20America%20I%20have%20seen_djvu.txt.

6. Lawrence Wright, *The Looming Tower: Al-Qaeda and the Road to 9/11* (New York: Vintage, 2007), 35.

7. Robert Spencer, "Sayyid Qutb and the Virginia Five," *Frontpage Mag*, December 18, 2009, www.frontpagemag.com/2009/robert-spencer/sayyid-qutb-and-the-virginia-five-by-robert-spencer/.

8. Wright, *The Looming Tower*, 36.

9. Hussein Aboubakr, "Where Are the Moderate Muslims?" PragerU.com, April 27, 2017, www.prageru.com/videos/where-are-moderate-muslims. Italics added for inflection.

10. George Orwell, *1984* (New York: Signet Classics/Penguin, 1977), 80.

11. Dov Lipman, "Meet My New Friend Hussein," *Jerusalem Post*, February 1, 2018, www.jpost.com/Opinion/Meet-my-new-friend-Hussein-540470.

12. Pew Research Center, "Chapter 1: Beliefs About Sharia," PewForum.org, April 30, 2013, www.pewforum.org/2013/04/30/the-worlds-muslims-religion-politics-society-beliefs-about-sharia. See also, Pew Research Center, "The World's Muslims: Religion, Politics and Society," PewForum.org, April 30, 2013, www.pewforum.org/2013/04/30/the-worlds-muslims-religion-politics-society-overview.

13. Rukmini Callimachi, "Paying Ransoms, Europe Bankrolls Qaeda Terror," *New York Times*, July 29, 2014, www.nytimes.com/2014/07/30/world/africa/ransoming-citizens-europe-becomes-al-qaedas-patron.html.

14. Daniel Pipes, "The Danger Within: Militant Islam in America," DanielPipes.org, November 2001, http://www.danielpipes.org/77/the-danger-within-militant-islam-in-america.

15. Daniel Pipes, *Nothing Abides: Perspectives on the Middle East and Islam* (London: Routledge, 2017), 240.

16. ADL staff, "The Council on American Islamic Relations (CAIR)," Anti-Defamation League, https://www.adl.org/education/resources/profiles/the-council-on-american-islamic-relations-cair.

17. Mimi Elkalla, "Judge Hears Arguments against San Diego Unified School District's Anti-bullying Plan," KGTV 10 News, July 17, 2018, www.10news.com/news/judge-hears-arguments-against-san-diego-unified-school

-district-s-anti-bullying-plan. Gary Warth, "Parents Sue SD Unified over Islamophobia Bullying Policy," *San Diego Union-Tribune*, May 23, 2017, www.sandiegouniontribune.com/news/education/sd-me-islamaphobia -lawsuit-20170523-story.html.

18. Andrew Kerr, "San Diego Schools Ordered to Reveal Correspondence with Muslim Advocacy Group," DailyCaller.com, March 7, 2018, http://dailycaller .com/2018/03/07/san-diego-schools-correspondence-muslim-group.

19. Ibid.

20. Seyla Benhabib, "Turkey Is About to Take Another Step toward Dictatorship," *Washington Post*, March 16, 2017, www.washingtonpost.com/news /democracy-post/wp/2017/03/16/turkey-is-about-to-take-another-step -toward-dictatorship/?utm_term=.9317a5364300.

21. Carlotta Gall, "Erdogan's Plan to Raise a 'Pious Generation' Divides Parents in Turkey," *New York Times*, June 18, 2018, www.nytimes.com/2018/06/18 /world/europe/erdogan-turkey-election-religious-schools.html.

22. Ibid.

23. Nadav Shragai, "Turkey's Target: The Temple Mount," *Jewish Journal*, July 5, 2018, https://jewishjournal.org/2018/07/05/turkeys-target-the-temple-mount. TOI Staff, "As Turkish Influence Grows in East Jerusalem, Arabs Said to Urge Israel to Act," *Times of Israel*, June 28, 2018, www.timesofisrael.com/as -turkish-influence-grows-in-east-jerusalem-arabs-said-to-urge-israel-to-act.

24. Hannah Lucinda Smith, "Turkish Strongman Erdogan Gets the Trump Fist -Bump Seal of Approval," *The Times* (UK), July 18, 2018, www.thetimes .co.uk/article/turkish-strongman-erdogan-gets-the-trump-fist-bump-seal-of -approval-kmk06zk2w. David Morgan, "Trump Fist-Bumped Turkish Leader Erdogan, Said He 'Does Things the Right Way'," CBS News, July 16, 2018, www.cbsnews.com/news/trump-fist-bumped-turkish-leader-erdogan-said-he -does-things-the-right-way.

CHAPTER 8: THE THIRD JIHAD IN "EURABIA"

1. Rabbi Abraham Cooper, "On Passover, We Can't Forget Mireille Knoll, Newly Murdered Holocaust Survivor, Victim of Anti-Semitism," FoxNews.com, March 29, 2018, www.foxnews.com/opinion/2018/03/29/on-passover -can-t-forget-mireille-knoll-newly-murdered-holocaust-survivor-victim -anti-semitism.html; Elian Peltier and Aurelien Breeden, "Mireille Knoll, Murdered Holocaust Survivor, Is Honored in Paris," *New York Times*, March 28, 2018, www.nytimes.com/2018/03/28/world/europe/mireille-knoll -murder-holocaust.html; Charles Bremner, "Two Charged With Killing 85-Year-Old Holocaust Survivor Mireille Knoll," *The Times*, March 28, 2018, www.thetimes.co.uk/article/two-charged-with-killing-85-year-old-holocaust -survivor-mireille-knoll-antisemitism-nz39s09jg; Keren Brosh, "Grandmother

Survived the Holocaust, Lost Her Life to Anti-Semitism," YnetNews.com, April 11, 2018, www.ynetnews.com/articles/0,7340,L-5226401,00.html.

2. "Religious Demographics of France," www.worldatlas.com/articles/religious -demographics-of-france.html.

3. Giulio Meotti, "Islam's 'Quiet Conquest' of Europe," GatestoneInstitute.org, August 10, 2016, https://www.gatestoneinstitute.org/8637/islam-europe -conquest.

4. Ibid.

5. Jon Henley, "Disabled Woman Set on Fire as Paris Riots Spread," *The Guardian*, November 4, 2005, www.theguardian.com/world/2005/nov/05 /france.jonhenley.

6. Patrick Jackson, "Creches Suffer in French Riots," BBC News, November 18, 2005, http://news.bbc.co.uk/2/hi/europe/4439734.stm.

7. Selwyn Duke, "Islam Is Taking Over Europe—'Without Swords, Without Guns, Without Conquest,'" Observer.com, January 25, 2017, http://observer .com/2017/01/muslim-population-europe-religion-growing-worldwide.

8. Harvard Divinity School staff, "Churches-to-Mosques Comment Sparks Debate in France," *Religious Literacy Project*, Harvard Divinity School, July 22, 2015, https://rlp.hds.harvard.edu/news/imam%E2%80%99s -churches-mosques-comment-sparks-debate-france.

9. Jamie Grierson, "Isis Follower Tried to Create Jihadist Child Army in East London," *The Guardian*, March 2, 2018, www.theguardian.com/uk -news/2018/mar/02/isis-follower-umar-haque-jihadist-child-army-east -london--radicalise. Clarion Project, "Teacher Planned to Raise 'Army' of Jihadi Children," ClarionProject.org, March 4, 2018, https://clarionproject .org/teacher-planned-raise-army-jihadi-children. Jamie Grierson, "Isis Supporter Jailed for Life for Trying to Build Child Army in London," *The Guardian*, March 27, 2018, www.theguardian.com/uk-news/2018 /mar/27/isis-supporter-umar-haque-jailed-build-child-army-london.

10. Grierson, "Isis Follower Tried to Create Jihadist Child Army."

11. Ibid.

12. Innes Bowen, "The End of One Law for All?," BBC News, November 28, 2006, http://news.bbc.co.uk/2/hi/uk_news/magazine/6190080.stm.

13. Times Staff, "Archbishop Calls for Sharia Elements in British Law," *Times of India*, February 9, 2008, https://timesofindia.indiatimes.com/world/uk /Archbishop-calls-for-sharia-elements-in-British-law/articleshow/2768181.cms.

14. Richard Edwards, "Sharia Courts Operating in Britain," *The Telegraph*, September 14, 2008, www.telegraph.co.uk/news/uknews/2957428/Sharia -law-courts-operating-in-Britain.html.

15. Justin Welby, *Reimagining Britain: Foundations for Hope* (London: Bloomsbury, 2018), 79, 82. Italics in the original.

16. Clarion Project, "Britain's Top Clergyman Warns Against Sharia Law," ClarionProject.org, February 27, 2018, https://clarionproject.org /britains-top-priest-warns-sharia-law/.

17. John F. Burns, "Britain Moves to Ban Islamic Group," *New York Times*, January 12, 2010, www.nytimes.com/2010/01/13/world/europe/13britain .html.

18. Lizzie Dearden, "Russia and Syria 'Weaponising' Refugee Crisis to Destabilise Europe, NATO Commander Claims," *Independent* (UK), March 3, 2016, www.independent.co.uk/news/world/middle-east/russia-and-syria -weaponising-refugee-crisis-to-destabilise-europe-nato-commander-claims -a6909241.html.

19. Ibid.

20. Ibid.

21. Audrey Gillan, "Militant Groups in the UK," *The Guardian*, June 18, 2002, www.theguardian.com/uk/2002/jun/19/religion.september11.

22. Oriana Fallaci, *The Force of Reason* (New York: Random House, 2006), 35.

23. Ibid., 36.

24. Ibid., 37.

25. Ibid., 25.

26. Mark Steyn, "She Said What She Thought," *The Atlantic*, December 2006, www.theatlantic.com/magazine/ archive/2006/12/she-said-what-she-thought/305377.

CHAPTER 9: COULD IT HAPPEN HERE?

1. Ibn Warraq, "One Imam, Multiple Messages," *National Review*, September 13, 2010, www.nationalreview.com/2010/09/one-imam-multiple -messages-ibn-warraq.

2. Andrew C. McCarthy, "Rauf's Dawa from the World Trade Center Rubble," *National Review*, July 24, 2010, www.nationalreview.com/2010/07/raufs -dawa-world-trade-center-rubble-andrew-c-mccarthy. Italics in the original.

3. Mark Tessler, *A History of the Israeli-Palestinian Conflict* (Bloomington: Indiana University Press, 1994), 21–22.

4. Dario Fernández-Morera, *The Myth of the Andalusian Paradise: Muslims, Christians, and Jews under Islamic Rule in Medieval Spain* (Wilmington, DE: ISI Books, 2016), 119.

5. Ibid., 120.

6. Avraham Yaakov Finkel, *The Essential Maimonides: Translations of the Rambam* (Northvale, NJ: Jason Aronson, Inc., 1996), 42.

7. Aluma Dankowitz, "Tariq Ramadan—Reformist or Islamist?," MEMRI.org, February 17, 2006, www.memri.org/reports/tariq-ramadan-%E2%80%93 -reformist-or-islamist.

8. Ibid.

9. Ibid. Ellipses in the original.

10. Ibid.

11. Ibid.

12. John 10:33

13. John 14:6, 9

14. Colossians 2:9

15. Matthew 28:19

16. John 10:14-15

17. Matthew 26:28

18. Ayaan Hirsi Ali, "Political Islam Is Today's Anti-American 'Long March through the Institutions,'" *The Federalist*, March 27, 2017, http://thefederalist.com/2017/03/27/political-islam-todays-anti-american-long-march-institutions.

19. Ayaan Hirsi Ali, *Heretic: Why Islam Needs a Reformation Now* (New York: HarperCollins, 2015), 33.

20. Ibid., 141.

21. Tunku Varadarajan, "Ayaan Hirsi Ali, Islam's Most Eloquent Apostate," *Wall Street Journal*, April 7, 2017, www.wsj.com/articles/ayaan-hirsi-ali-islams-most-eloquent-apostate-1491590469.

22. Hirsi Ali, *Heretic*, 3.

23. Hirsi Ali, "Political Islam."

24. "Jefferson's Letter to the Danbury Baptists: The Final Letter, as Sent," *Library of Congress Information Bulletin*, June 1998, www.loc.gov/loc/lcib/9806/danpre.html.

25. Leviticus 19:33-34

26. Matthew 25:35

27. Amy Sherman, "Did the U.S. Education Department Introduce an Islamic Indoctrination Program for Public Schools?," PolitiFact.com, April 5, 2017, www.politifact.com/florida/statements/2017/apr/05/volusia-county-republican-party/did-us-department-education-introduce-islamic-indo.

28. Online transcript of "Hajj, Part I," *Access Islam*, Thirteen.org, original airdate: March 27, 1998, www.thirteen.org/edonline/accessislam/video_130watch.html.

29. Todd Starnes, "Lawsuit: Public School Forced My Child to Convert to Islam," FoxNews.com, January 29, 2016, www.foxnews.com/opinion/2016/01/29/lawsuit-public-school-forced-my-child-to-convert-to-islam.html.

30. *Islamic Beliefs, Practices, and Cultures* (Tarrytown, NY: Marshall Cavendish Corp., 2011), 73.

31. Emma Brown, "This Marine Vet Was Banned from His Kid's School after Objecting to Islam Lessons," *Washington Post*, February 23, 2016. Underlining in the original; www.washingtonpost.com/news/education/wp/2016/02/23/this-marine-vet-was-banned-from-his-kids-school-after-objecting-to-islam-lessons.

32. Starnes, "Lawsuit: Public School Forced My Child to Convert to Islam."
33. Ibid.
34. Ibid.

CHAPTER 10: THE SECULAR-ISLAMIST ALLIANCE

1. *Jerusalem Embassy Act of 1995*, Public Law 104–45, 104th Congress, sec. 3, www.congress.gov/104/plaws/publ45/PLAW-104publ45.pdf.
2. Bill Chappell, "55 Palestinian Protesters Killed, Gaza Officials Say, as U.S. Opens Jerusalem Embassy," National Public Radio, May 14, 2018, www.npr.org/sections/thetwo-way/2018/05/14/610934534/18-palestinian-protesters-die-gaza-officials-say-as-u-s-opens-jerusalem-embassy.
3. Tovah Lazaroff, "Haley: Hamas Must Stop Using Gaza Children as Cannon Fodder," *Jerusalem Post*, April 26, 2018, www.jpost.com/Arab-Israeli-Conflict/Haley-Hamas-must-stop-using-Gaza-children-as-cannon-fodder-552832.
4. Tricia McDermott, "Arafat's Billions," *60 Minutes*, CBS News, November 7, 2003, www.cbsnews.com/news/arafats-billions.
5. Associated Press, "International Investors Hope for Visible Returns in Gaza," *Haaretz*, October 14, 2005, www.haaretz.com/1.4877897.
6. World Bank, "A Sustainable Recovery in Gaza Is Not Foreseen Without Trade," World Bank press release, March 15, 2018, www.worldbank.org/en/news/press-release/2018/03/15/a-sustainable-recovery-in-gaza-is-not-foreseen-without-trade.
7. Tzipi Hotovely, "Where Does All That Aid for Palestinians Go?," *Wall Street Journal*, January 24, 2016, www.wsj.com/articles/where-does-all-that-aid-for-palestinians-go-1453669813. Italics added.
8. Hunter Stuart, "How a Pro-Palestinian American Reporter Changed His Views on Israel and the Conflict," *Jerusalem Post*, February 15, 2017, www.jpost.com/Jerusalem-Report/A-view-from-the-frontlines-480829.
9. Ibid.
10. Michael Prell, *Underdogma: How America's Enemies Use Our Love for the Underdog to Trash American Power* (Dallas: BenBella Books, 2011), 13, 41–42.
11. Jeff Baillon, "Millions of Dollars in Suitcases Fly Out of MSP, but Why?," Fox9.com, May 13, 2018, www.fox9.com/news/investigators/millions-of-dollars-in-suitcases-fly-out-of-msp-but-why.
12. "The Pernicious Myth of the Oppressed European Muslim," *Investor's Business Daily*, March 24, 2016, www.investors.com/politics/editorials/the-pernicious-myth-of-the-oppressed-european-muslim.
13. Tom Godfrey, "Harems Pay Off for Muslims," *Toronto Sun*, December 30, 2008, https://web.archive.org/web/20161117174632/http://www.torontosun.com/news/torontoandgta/2008/12/31/7891231.html.
14. Lucy Ballinger and Dan Newling, "Guilty? It's a Badge of Honour Say Muslim Hate Mob (and Because We're on Benefits, the State Will Pay Our Costs),"

Daily Mail, January 12, 2010, www.dailymail.co.uk/news/article-1242335
/Muslims-called-British-soldiers-rapists-cowards-scum-exercising-freedom
-speech-court-hears.html.

15. Robert Johnson, "Muslim Preacher Tells Followers Getting Welfare Cash for
    Holy Wars Is Easy and Right," *Business Insider*, February 18, 2013, www
    .businessinsider.com/anjem-choudary-muslim-preacher-explains-government
    -assistance-to-fund-jihad-holy-war-2013-2. See also, "Anjem Choudary How
    to Claim Jihad Seekers Allowance," YouTube, January 16, 2018, www.youtube
    .com/watch?v=6xGDg01QPJc.

16. Peter Hasson, "Keith Ellison Wears T-Shirt Calling for Open Borders,"
    Daily Caller, May 7, 2018, http://dailycaller.com/2018/05/07/keith
    -ellison-open-borders-shirt.

17. Victor Davis Hanson, "Why Borders Matter—and a Borderless World Is a
    Fantasy," *Los Angeles Times*, July 31, 2016, www.latimes.com/opinion/op-ed
    /la-oe-hanson-borders-20160731-snap-story.html.

18. Lyndsay Winkley, "When It Comes to Murder Rates, No Big City Is Safer
    than San Diego," *San Diego Union Tribune*, September 25, 2017, www
    .sandiegouniontribune.com/news/public-safety/sd-me-fbi-crime-20170925
    -story.html. Jessica Dillinger, "The Most Dangerous Cities in the World,"
    WorldAtlas.com, April 25, 2018, www.worldatlas.com/articles/most
    -dangerous-cities-in-the-world.html.

19. Stephen Haggard, "North Korea by Night: Satellite Images Shed New Light
    on the Secretive State," *The Guardian*, April 23, 2014, www.cbsnews.com
    /pictures/north-korea-hermit-country-space-photos.

20. Deroy Murdock, "Border Wall Needed for National Security,
    Counterterrorism," *National Review*, January 31, 2018, www.nationalreview
    .com/2018/01/illegal-immigrants-terrorism-border-wall-could-help-prevent
    -attacks.

21. Steve Brusk, "Perry Greets Obama, Delivers Border Message," CNN Politics,
    August 9, 2010, http://politicalticker.blogs.cnn.com/2010/08/09/perry
    -greets-obama-delivers-immigration-message.

22. Murdock, "Border Wall Needed."

23. Patrick J. Hayes, ed., *The Making of Modern Immigration: An Encyclopedia of
    People and Ideas*, vol. 1 (Santa Barbara, CA: ABC-CLIO, 2012), 34.

24. Thomas Sowell, @ThomasSowell, Twitter.com, May 16, 2018,
    https://twitter.com/thomassowell/status/996732570179076097?lang=en.

25. "Man Arrested at New Mexico Compound Is Son of Imam with Possible
    Link to 1993 World Trade Center Bombing," CBS/Associated Press,
    August 8, 2018, www.cbsnews.com/news/siraj-wahhaj-arrested-amalia
    -new-mexico-father-imam-possible-link-1993-world-trade-center-bombing
    -court-documents.

26. Emanuella Grinberg, Scott McLean, and Sara Weisfeldt, "New Mexico Compound Suspects Were on a Violent Mission, Prosecutors Say. But the Defense Sees It Differently," CNN.com, August 14, 2018, www.cnn.com /2018/08/13/us/new-mexico-compund-suspects/index.html.

27. Elizabeth Chuck, "Bail Reform: Why Didn't Judge Detain New Mexico Compound Suspects?" NBCNews.com, August 14, 2018, www.nbcnews.com /news/us-news/bail-reform-why-didn-t-judge-detain-new-mexico-compound -n900641.

28. Tabassum Zakaria, "General Casey: Diversity Shouldn't Be Casualty of Fort Hood," Reuters, November 8, 2009, http://blogs.reuters.com /talesfromthetrail/2009/11/08/general-casey-diversity-shouldnt-be-casualty-of -fort-hood.

29. Michael Daly, "Note Purple Hearts: Nidal Hasan's Murders Termed 'Workplace Violence' by U.S.," *The Daily Beast*, August 6, 2013, www.thedailybeast.com/nidal-hasans-murders-termed-workplace-violence -by-us.

30. For information about the Independent Inquiry into Child Sexual Abuse, see www.iicsa.org.uk.

31. Tim Ross, "Labour MPs: Left Ignored Sex Abuse," *The Telegraph*, August 30, 2014, www.telegraph.co.uk/news/politics/labour/11065878/Labour-MPs -Left-ignored-sex-abuse.html?fb.

32. David Harris, "UK Ignored Sexual Abuse of 1,400 Girls by Muslim Gangs," ClarionProject.org, August 31, 2014, https://clarionproject.org/uk-officials -ignored-sexual-abuse-1400-girls-16-yrs-9.

CHAPTER 11: THE KEY TO SURVIVAL

1. Abraham Lincoln, "The Perpetuation of Our Political Institutions: Address Before the Young Men's Lyceum of Springfield, Illinois," January 27, 1838, www.abrahamlincolnonline.org/lincoln/speeches/lyceum.htm.

2. Ernest Hemingway, *The Sun Also Rises* (New York: Scribner, 1926, 2006 edition), 141.

3. Andrew Gilligan and Alex Spillius, "Barack Obama Adviser Says Sharia Law Is Misunderstood," *The Telegraph* (UK), October 8, 2009; www.telegraph.co.uk /news/worldnews/barackobama/6274387/Obama-adviser-says-Sharia-Law-is -misunderstood.html.

4. Ryan Mauro, "A Window on the Muslim Brotherhood in America: An Annotated Interview with DHS Advisor Mohamed Elibiary," Center for Security Policy, October 6, 2013, www.centerforsecuritypolicy.org/wp -content/uploads/2013/09/Elibiary-Occasional-Paper-1001.pdf.

5. Story adapted from Michael Youssef, "Fatima's Story: 'I'm Not Scared Anymore,'" Leading The Way, April 10, 2017, www.ltw.org/read /articles/2017/04/fatimas-story-i-am-not-scared-anymore.

6. Alan Heimert, *Religion and the American Mind: From the Great Awakening to the Revolution* (Eugene, OR: Wipf and Stock, 1966; reissued 2006), 14.

7. John 8:31-32

8. Jude 1:3

9. James 4:8

10. Revelation 3:16

11. Revelation 3:17

12. Revelation 3:18

13. Psalm 19:7

14. John 15:7

15. David R. Mains, *What's Wrong with Lukewarm?* (Elgin, IL: David C. Cook, 1987), 18.

16. 1 Samuel 15:22

17. A. W. Tozer, "Don't Substitute Praying for Obeying," in *Tozer on Christian Leadership: A 365-Day Devotional*, comp. Ronald Eggert (Camp Hill, PA: WingSpread, 2001), September 23.

18. Isaiah 57:15

19. Psalm 139:23-24

20. Matthew 18:20

21. Matthew 16:16, 18

22. Quoted in Charles Simpson, *Walking in the Footsteps of David Wilkerson: The Journey and Reflections of a Spiritual Son* (Shippensburg, PA: Destiny Image, 2018), Kindle edition.

23. Andrew Murray, *The Essential Works of Andrew Murray* (Uhrichsville, OH: Barbour, 2008), 1012.

24. 2 Chronicles 7:12-14

25. 2 Chronicles 7:14, author paraphrase.

26. Psalm 85:6

CHAPTER 12: DON'T BE AFRAID

1. Winston Spencer Churchill, *The River War*, first edition, vol. II (London: Longmans, Green, 1899), 250.

2. Hilaire Belloc, *The Great Heresies* (Freeport, NY: Books for Libraries Press, 1938), 127.

3. See 2 Timothy 1:7.

4. Mark Thompson, interview by Timothy Garton Ash, Free Speech Debate, https://freespeechdebate.com/media/mark-thompson-talks-religion /#comments. A transcript of the interview may be found online at http:// freespeechdebate.com/wp-content/uploads/2012/03/Mark-Thompson1.pdf.

5. Ibid.

6. Ibid.

7. Joshua 1:2-9

8. Psalm 118:6
9. Isaiah 43:1
10. John 14:27
11. 2 Timothy 1:7
12. 1 John 4:18
13. Matthew 28:20
14. Deuteronomy 31:6, 8; Joshua 1:5
15. John 14:27
16. 2 Corinthians 4:4
17. See Romans 13:1-4.
18. Ephesians 6:12
19. Ephesians 6:14
20. John 8:44
21. Ephesians 6:14
22. Ephesians 6:15
23. Ephesians 6:16
24. Ephesians 6:17
25. Ibid.